EDWARD SRI

NO GREATER LOVE

A BIBLICAL WALK THROUGH CHRIST'S PASSION

ASCENSION

West Chester, Pennsylvania

Ascension
Post Office Box 1990
West Chester, PA 19380
1-800-376-0520
ascensionpress.com

Printed in the United States of America

ISBN 978-1-945179-73-0

To Fortunata Bonini, my grandmother

CONTENTS

ACKNOWLEDGMENTS

I am thankful to my students and colleagues throughout the years at Benedictine College, the Augustine Institute, and FOCUS (Fellowship of Catholic University Students) for various conversations about the Passion narratives that have enriched my thoughts on these passages. I give special thanks to the Missionaries of Charity for various retreats they have invited me to lead on the Passion narratives and the theology of the Cross. Their prayers for me and insights on Christ's passion have blessed me and my work on this project. Special thanks also goes to Joe Hensler and friends at Pax Christi for our small Bible study group on Christ's passion. I also am grateful for the good people at Ascension, especially Matt Pinto and John Harden for inviting me to do this project, and for John, Jen Eckenrode, and the editorial and video teams that helped make this a better book and video study program. Finally, I am most grateful for my bride, Beth, for her encouraging me to do this project that has been on my heart for many years and her continued prayers and support throughout the work.

INTRODUCTION:
"The Passion of a True Love"

Olive trees on the Mount of Olives

God is a lover with all the passion of a true love.[1]

—Pope Benedict XVI

On the Mount of Olives overlooking Jerusalem, there is a patch of olive trees on a site traditionally believed to be the garden of Gethsemane—the place where Jesus came to pray the night before he died. The olive trees themselves are about 900 years old, and the root systems may go back all the way to the time of Jesus. These small sacred grounds, tucked away amid the noisy, busy streets of modern-day Jerusalem, remain one of the few areas in the city that gives us a small glimpse into the Jerusalem of Jesus' day.

I like to take pilgrims here because, when we draw near to these olive trees, we come in contact with something from the life of Jesus. We stand on the same mountain where Jesus began his passion, and we can begin to picture the place where he prayed in his agony. Entering the sites of Christ's passion like this can be

---

[1] Benedict XVI, encyclical letter, *Deus Caritas Est (God Is Love)*, 10.

a profoundly moving experience. Suddenly, we come to a deeper realization of how *real* our faith is. Jesus is not just a doctrine, a picture in my living room, an image on a crucifix, or a figure from a book written a long time ago. He is a real person who made real choices and who came right here to this place to begin his passion and give up his life for me. I am standing where he stood—the God who became man. I am walking in his footsteps. He sweat drops of blood for me here. And he did all this so I can be in a close friendship with him today. It can be overwhelming to take all this in all at once, and such an experience often sparks a renewed encounter with the living Jesus.

But we do not have to go all the way to the Holy Land to have such an experience. We can encounter that same Jesus through the inspired Scriptures whether we are in Sydney, Toronto, New York, or small towns like Freemont, Nebraska and Atchison, Kansas. And that is what I hope to do in this book—bring you, personally, in closer contact with the living Jesus by entering deeper into the Gospel accounts of his passion and death. Think of this book as a *biblical* pilgrimage through the last hours of Christ's life. We are going to walk step-by-step with Jesus on his journey from Gethsemane to the Cross and unpack the biblical background—the history, the prophecies, and most especially, the ways Jesus is inviting us to walk more closely with him today.

In a sense, I want to take you in a "time machine" back to that first century Jewish world of Jesus. Many of us have heard about Jesus agonizing in a garden and being scourged at a pillar and nailed to a cross. But imagine if you had never heard these stories before. Imagine if you were a Jew in the first century hearing these stories for the first time. Imagine if you were Peter or John or one of the other apostles encountering these events as they originally unfolded. What would these experiences have meant to you?

A Biblical Minefield

As we journey with Christ through his passion, one thing we will quickly notice is how every detail in these Gospel narratives is there for a reason. Do not be fooled, thinking small points like the "hyssop" used to bring Jesus his last drink of vinegary wine can't be very significant (see John 19:29). As we will see, that tiny reference would be huge for the Jews in the first century, recalling the hyssop their ancestors used in Egypt to mark their doorposts with the blood of the Passover lambs. John's Gospel mentions the "hyssop" at Calvary in the context of the Passover feast in order to proclaim that Jesus is the true Passover Lamb being sacrificed to save us. Similarly, do not think that the small points about Christ's unbroken bones and his body being pierced in his side and then laid in a garden tomb are insignificant background details to the story. Each point brings to mind various prophecies in the Jewish Scriptures and the hopes that people had for what God would come to do for them.

Walking through the narratives of Christ's passion is like walking through a biblical mine field. It is as if at every step of the way, Old Testament prophecies, messianic expectations, and connections to our Christian faith today are wonderfully blowing up all around us. We will see that practically every word in these Gospel accounts of Christ's passion is charged with great significance. Just the names of various places (such as Mount of Olives, Gethsemane, and Jerusalem) as well as the names of various characters (such as Barabbas, Joseph of Arimathea, and Simon of Cyrene) give important clues as to the role they play in God's larger plan of salvation. Even the mere mention of someone's posture is important: The high priest *standing up*, Jesus *falling down with his face to the ground*, Jesus *turning to look at Peter*— each expressing key turning points in the scene and serving as windows into the soul of the person at that moment.

This journey will also give us a deeper appreciation of what Jesus endured for our sake, from his agony in the garden to his death on Calvary. We will also address some of the puzzling words Jesus speaks during his passion, such as:

> "Father, if it is possible, let this cup pass from me" (Matthew 26:39, NAB). (Was Jesus thinking of backing out at the last minute?)

> "Daughters of Jerusalem, do not weep for me, but weep for yourselves and for your children" (Luke 23:28). (Doesn't that seem a harsh thing to say to women who are compassionately weeping for him?)

> "My God, my God why have you forsaken me?" (Matthew 27:46). (Was Jesus really forsaken by the Father on Good Friday?)

> "You have said so" (Matthew 26:64). (What does *that* mean?)

Most of all, as St. John Paul II once said, the passion of Christ is "*the culmination of the revelation of God's love.*"[2] But this is not an amazing love that is simply meant to be admired from afar. Jesus does not want our applause. He wants our hearts. He wants to transform our hearts with this love. So, as we walk through Christ's passion, we will consider how we can live his example of love in our own daily lives. After all, these are not just stories from a long time ago. Jesus wants us to make them our own. He wants to re-live the love story of his passion in us. For when we allow Christ to do that, we discover a greater love than the world has ever known. Indeed, as Jesus himself said, "Greater love has no man than this, that a man lay down his life for his friends" (John 15:13).

Where "The Passion" Got Its Name

Have you ever wondered why Christians described the events leading up to Jesus' death on Good Friday as "the passion" of Christ? On a basic level, the English word "passion" is derived from the Latin word *passio*, meaning suffering. The expression,

---

[2] St. John Paul II, apostolic letter, *Rosarium Virginis Mariae* (On the Rosary of the Virgin Mary), (October 16, 2002), 22, original emphasis.

therefore, came to describe the afflictions Christ endured for our sins in the last day of his life.

In our modern era, some have seen an additional meaning. Today, the word passion in English can describe an intense feeling or emotion. According to Webster's Dictionary, "passion" means "a strong feeling of enthusiasm or excitement for something." Along these lines, people sometimes describe themselves as doing something passionately—with all their heart, with full commitment, drive, and purpose. That sense might also come into play with understanding Christ's determination to give his life for our sins. He is not a passive victim, taken by surprise and forced to endure a horrific death. He is the one who said to the Father, "Not my will, but yours be done" (Luke 22;42), and he chose to drink to the last drop from the cup of his suffering, all for the sake of our salvation.

Pope Benedict XVI, however, takes us even deeper. In his work *God Is Love,* he describes Christ's passion in the context of passionate love. But here we must be clear: He is not talking about a fallen, human passionate love, which on its own is merely a kind of intoxication, in which we are swept away by our emotions, romantic feelings, and sensual desires. Such a love is inward-looking, focusing primarily on one's own feelings and desires—on what I get out of the other person. Such a self-centered love cannot endure.

God does have a passionate love for his people. He is "a lover with all the passion of a true love," Pope Benedict says. But his passionate love for the human family expresses itself in a higher form of love summed up by the Greek word *agape,* which is a total, committed sacrificial love. *Agape* love is outward-looking, seeking what is best for the other person and even willing to suffer and sacrifice for that person's good. Think about how *agape* love is seen most perfectly in God's love for us. Even though we turned away from God in sin and even though according to justice, we have been separated from God and have a debt to pay for our sin, God's passionate love drove him to become one of us and pay that debt on our behalf. So much did God love us that he did not want us to remain separated from him forever. He went to every measure to seek us out. He even was willing to become one of us and die for us, so that we could be reunited with him. As Benedict XVI explains, "God's passionate love for his people … is so great that it turns God against himself, his love against his justice … so great is God's love for man that by becoming man he follows him even into death, and so reconciles justice and love."[3]

Think of the passion of Christ as the sufferings Jesus endured for our sins. Think of it as his passionate determination to reconcile us to himself. But Benedict XVI invites us to think of it also as *the passion of a lover.* God's passionate love for his people expresses itself as *agape* as Jesus loves us so much, he is willing to enter our suffering and sacrifice himself for our sins. And he wants our hearts to be transformed by this same perfect *agape* love which he models for us every step of the way from Gethsemane to the Cross.

More Than Suffering

Sometimes when Christians think about Christ's sacrifice on Calvary, they focus primarily on the suffering he endured. Catholic Tradition, however, emphasizes that Christ's love is what gives the Cross its redeeming value. Certainly, it is a total self-giving love that is expressed poignantly through sacrifice and suffering, but love—not the amount of blood, pain, or torture—is at the center. To paraphrase St. Catherine: The nails could not have held him fast to the Cross, if love had not held him there first.[4]

> The nails could not have held him fast to the Cross, if love had not held him there first.

---

[3] Benedict XVI, *Deus Caritas Est (God Is Love), 10.*

[4] Augusta Theodosia Drane, *The History of St. Catherine of Sienna and Her Companions* (London: Burns and Oats, 1887), 137.

Others sometimes focus on the innocent Jesus stepping in and taking on the wrath of God that should have been poured out on us, the guilty ones. Think about that. Picture a child doing something terribly wrong and about to receive a spanking from his father. At the last second, a sibling steps in and says, "No, Father, let him go. Spank me instead." The father looks at the innocent child ... then the guilty one ... then back at the innocent child and says, "I don't care who I punish. I just need to pour out my wrath on someone!" He then proceeds to give the innocent child the spanking that the guilty one deserved.

How would that possibly solve the problem? How does such arbitrary punishment bring about a loving reconciliation between father and son? Similarly, a God who punishes the innocent instead of the guilty would not be a God of mercy or justice. St. John Paul II once explained that what gives the Cross its "redemptive value is not the material fact that an innocent person has suffered the chastisement deserved by the guilty and that justice has thus been in some way satisfied." Rather, the saving power of the Cross "comes from the fact that the innocent Jesus, out of pure love, entered into solidarity with the guilty and thus transformed their situation from within."[5] In other words, what makes the cross redemptive is not that fact that punishment has been inflicted on an innocent victim or that God's anger has been appeased. Rather, at the heart of the saving power of the cross is Christ's unique total gift of himself in love. As the *Catechism of the Catholic Church* explains, "It is love 'to the end' (John 13:1) that confers on Christ's sacrifice its value as redemption and reparation, as atonement and satisfaction" (CCC 616).

Indeed, Christ's gift of love on Calvary is utterly unique in human history, far surpassing what any ordinary human could do.

---

[5]   St. John Paul II, General Audience, October 26, 1988, in *Jesus, Son and Savior: A Catechesis on the Creed* (Boston: Pauline, 1996), 445.

Because he is fully human, Jesus can represent the human family and offer an act of love to the Father on our behalf. Because Jesus is also fully divine, his act of love takes on infinite value and can bridge the infinite gap between us and God that was caused by our sin. As St. Bernard of Clairvaux is often attributed as saying, "The smallest drop of Christ's blood would have been enough to have redeemed all mankind." That is why only Christ's sacrificial gift of love can reconcile us to the Father.[6]

This first part of this book will walk through Christ's passion from his agony in the garden through his death and burial. The second part will focus on what is known as the Seven Last Words of Christ—the seven brief sayings of Jesus from the cross. While our walk through Christ's passion draws on all four Gospels, we recognize each writer has his own particular audience and message in mind, so each account often has distinctive emphases. We do not intend to offer a precise play-by-play reconstruction of each point in each scene. Instead, our aim is to bring people into a deeper encounter with Jesus in his Passion through the various insights of the four Gospel writers.

Though this book can be used as part of a video study program by the same name for parishes, small groups, and families, the work stands on its own and does not require additional background or resources. Questions at the end of each chapter can be used for personal reflection or group discussion.

---

[6]   For more on Christ's sacrifice on the Cross, see Edward Sri, *Love Unveiled: The Catholic Faith Explained* (San Francisco: Ignatius, 2015), 83-92.

Chapter One

THE GREAT BATTLE

View of Jerusalem from the Mount of Olives, Guiding Star Pilgrimages, LLC

Mel Gibson's classic film *The Passion of the Christ* begins in Gethsemane with an eerie satanic figure sending a serpent to attack Jesus during his agony in the garden. Though such a scene is the fruit of artistic imagination and not explicitly narrated in the New Testament, the idea of Satan mounting his final assault on Christ at this moment is, in fact, rooted in Scripture, especially in the Gospel of Luke.

All four Gospels emphasize the true enemy of Christ is not the chief priests, Herod, or Rome but rather a much fiercer opponent: the devil. Three of the Gospels—Matthew, Mark, and Luke—make this point right at the start of Christ's public ministry, telling how the first battle Jesus faces is against the devil, who tempts him three times in the desert. Only Luke, however, gives a clear foreshadowing of how the devil will be coming back for more. After narrating how Jesus successfully resists Satan's temptations, Luke notes that "the devil departed from him *until the opportune time*" (Luke 4:13, emphasis added). This implies that Satan will square off against Jesus some other time in the future. Jesus may have won this first battle, but the war is not over. The devil will strike again at "the opportune time."

That "opportune time" has now arrived in the garden of Gethsemane.

Throughout his public ministry, Jesus faced many smaller skirmishes with the devil's power. Every time he raised the dead, forgave sins, and expelled demons, he was confronting the powers of darkness. But leading up to this night in Gethsemane, Luke's Gospel signals that something is significantly different. Satan is preparing to return in full force, mounting his final attack on Christ.

First, Luke informs us that "Satan entered into Judas" as he went to the chief priests to discuss how to betray Jesus (Luke 22:3-4). Next, at the Last Supper, Jesus warns the disciples, "Satan demanded to have you, that he might sift you like wheat" (Luke 22:31). Satan is clearly on the move. One by one, he is picking off Jesus' own disciples.

The devil is also stirring Christ's enemies to make their move against him. When Judas comes with the chief priests, elders, and soldiers to arrest him, Jesus points out how a more sinister force is at work. He associates this group with "the power of darkness"—imagery associated with Satan in the New Testament (see Acts 26:18). The message is clear: the chief priests, elders, and soldiers have become instruments of Satan against Jesus. Jesus says to them, "Have you come out as against a robber, with swords and clubs? When I was with you day after day in the temple, you did not lay hands on me. But this is your hour, and the power of darkness" (Luke 22:53).

All this tells us something very important about Christ's passion. As the story unfolds, we will see Jesus be betrayed by Judas, denied by Peter, slapped by the chief priests, mocked by Herod, scourged by Roman soldiers, and sent off to be crucified by Pilate. Yet, as we start our walk with Jesus through his passion, we must keep in mind who the real enemy is and what is really at stake. This is not just a sad story about a good man being treated horribly by his friends and enemies. This is the great cosmic battle—the ultimate showdown between good and evil, light and darkness, the woman's seed and the serpent, God and the devil. And the very salvation of all humanity depends on the outcome of this battle.

The Mount of Olives

"And he came out and went as was his custom to the Mount of Olives" (Luke 22:39).

The fact that Jesus came to the Mount of Olives at the start of his passion is significant. Jesus had prayed on mountains at other times (see Luke 6:12, 9:28). However, the Mount of Olives has special importance in Scripture. There are six references in the Old Testament to this mountain range that runs parallel to Jerusalem on the east. One explicit mention of the "Mount of Olives" is in the apocalyptic prophecy of Zechariah 14. It foretells how the feet of the Lord "will stand on the Mount of Olives" for the final battle against the nations who oppress God's people after which arrives the great blessings that come in the day of the Lord (Zechariah 14:3-4, 6-9). When Jesus stepped foot on the Mount of Olives to begin his agony in the garden, he likely had this prophecy in mind. For that great battle Zechariah foretold is about to begin as Jesus squares off against the ultimate enemy—the devil.

But there was something more. When Jesus came to the Mount of Olives this night, he was likely remembering another king who came to this same place to weep and pray when he was betrayed about a thousand years before Christ—King David.

In the only other explicit reference to the Mount of Olives in the Old Testament, 2 Samuel 15 tells how David fled to this same mountain when his son Absalom led a revolt against him with the help of David's trusted counselor, a man named Ahithophel.

Several details of this story are noteworthy: When Ahithophel deserted David, the king "went forth" (*exerchesthai*) from the city of Jerusalem (2 Samuel 15:16), crossed the "brook Kidron" (2 Samuel 15:23), "went up the ascent of the Mount of Olives weeping" (2 Samuel 15:30), and prayed there (2 Samuel 15:31).

Notice the parallels with Jesus. Like David, Jesus *"went forth"* (*eiserchesthai)* to cross the "brook flowing Kidron" (John 18:1)[7] to arrive at the *Mount of Olives* (see Mark 14:26; Luke 22:39) where he *prayed* in his agony, being sorrowful even unto death. Like David who came to the Mount of Olives in the context of having been betrayed by Ahithophel, Jesus goes here as he awaits his own betrayal by Judas. Both Ahithophel and Judas betrayed their king. And the fact that Judas will eventually hang himself adds to the parallelism, for there are only two people in all of Scripture to die such a death: Ahithophel and Judas (see 2 Samuel 17:23; Matthew 27:5). David's suffering on this same Mount of Olives foreshadows what the true King, Jesus, will face at the start of his passion.

DAVID	JESUS
Betrayed by his counselor Ahithophel (see 2 Samuel 15:12)	Betrayed by his apostle Judas (see Luke 22:48)
"went forth" from Jerusalem (2 Samuel 15:16)	"went forth" from Jerusalem (John 18:1)
Crossed the Kidron (see 2 Samuel 15:23)	Crossed the Kidron (see John 18:1)
Went up to the Mount of Olives and prayed (see 2 Samuel 15:30-31)	Went up to the Mount of Olives and prayed (see Mark 14:26, 32; Luke 22:39-41)
Ahithophel hangs himself (see 2 Samuel 17:23)	Judas hangs himself (see Matthew 27:5)

---

7   See Raymond Brown, *The Gospel According to John XIII-XXI* (Garden City, NY: Doubleday, 1970), 806.

The Mount of Olives

Precisely where on the Mount of Olives Jesus went to pray, we do not know for certain. Scripture tells us it was in a garden (see John 18:1) in a place known as "Gethsemane"—which is based on the Semitic word for oil press (*gat shemen*). The name suggests that this garden probably had olive trees and an oil press in it. Since the fourth century, a site on the lower part of the Mount of Olives has been revered as the location where Jesus' agony took place, either on a rock formation that pilgrims venerate today in the Church of All Nations, or a cave nearby that may have housed an oil press.

Gethsemane: A Window into Jesus' Soul

As soon as Jesus arrived at Gethsemane, he faced an intense ordeal. The Gospels make this clear in five small details that serve as a window into Jesus' soul and the agony he experienced in the garden.

First, Mark points out that Jesus "began to be greatly distraught" (*ekthambeisthai*). This word describes no ordinary agitation (e.g., I'm not feeling well, I'm stuck in traffic, my favorite team lost), but a profound distress that could even manifest itself physically before a horrifying event (see Mark 14:33). Think of Jesus experiencing the kind of intense anguish described by the suffering man in Psalm 55: "I am overcome by trouble, I am distraught by the noise of the enemy ... My heart is in anguish within me, the terrors of death have fallen upon me. Fear and trembling come upon me, and horror overwhelms me" (Psalm 55:2-5).

Second, Jesus makes a remarkable statement: "My soul is very sorrowful, even to death" (Mark 14:34). Such words are completely unprecedented for Jesus as he opens his heart to talk about what is happening inside him, how the mere thought of his passion is affecting him personally. On previous occasions, Jesus

> Sometimes a friend becoming a foe can be more painful than death itself.

had talked about his upcoming death, but never so directly regarding how his own soul was going to be greatly troubled by it (see Mark 8:31, 9:31, and 10:33-34).

The expression describes a person being pushed to the limits with grief, experiencing almost unbearable suffering. As Jesus anticipates his passion and death and the scattering of his own disciples, it "is enough to kill him, and he will ask God to be delivered from such a fate."[8] Jesus' words recall the many Psalms of Lament, such as "My eye is wasted from grief, my soul and body also. For my life is spent with sorrow" (Psalm 31:10-11) and "My soul is cast down within me" (Psalm 42:6).[9] Various psalms like these feature a righteous man facing suffering and persecution and having feelings of hopelessness and abandonment. As the man expresses to God his fears and sorrows, a profound hope emerges as he also expresses his confidence that the Lord ultimately will rescue him and set things right.

The Old Testament passage that perhaps most reflects this moment is found in the book of Sirach, where the expression describes a kind of suffering that can be among the most painful in life—the suffering one experiences when a friend has turned against you. Sirach 37:2 states, "Is it not grief to the death when your companion and friend is turned to enemy?" Sometimes a friend becoming a foe can be more painful than death itself.

This sheds much light on what Jesus was suffering in the Garden of Gethsemane when his friend, Judas, was coming with the

---

8   Raymond Brown, *Death of the Messiah* (New York: Doubleday, 1994), 1:156.

9   The expression in Greek is closest to the thrice repeated refrain in the Psalms 41-42 LXX, "Why are you cast down, O my soul…?"

chief priests and elders to arrest him. Jesus' agony in the garden was not only about the intense physical pain he would experience in his crucifixion the next day or even the weight of the sins of humanity he was about to bear. His soul being "very sorrowful, even to death" also points to what his friend Judas was about to do: betray him. Perhaps more than the torturous physical suffering of the Cross, Judas' betrayal—the friend who is "turned to enemy"—may have been what caused Jesus the greatest sorrow that night.

No Ordinary Prayer Time

Third, Jesus withdrew from his apostles to pray on his own. Upon arriving at the garden with his disciples, Jesus told them to watch and pray while he goes a little further to pray. He initially took Peter, James, and John with him, but now separates himself even from these three, "going a little further" still to pray on his own (Mark 14:35). Luke describes it as "about a stone's throw" away. Separating one's self for prayer is a common theme in the Old Testament (see Genesis 22:5; Exodus 19:17; 24:14) and Jesus himself often sought solitude for prayer (see Mark 1:35, 6:46; Luke 6:12).

The Gospels, however, make clear that this is no ordinary prayer time for Jesus. Luke notes that Jesus suddenly "withdrew from them" (Luke 22:41). In classical Greek, the verb used here for "withdrew" (*apospan*) has the meaning of tearing away violently. It can literally be translated "he was pulled away from them."[10] The force of the verb describes the intensity of what Jesus is facing in the garden as he tears away from his disciples to enter into his agony. Moreover, there is only one other place in the entire New Testament where this verb is used to describe someone personally withdrawing from others. Acts 21:1 depicts Paul tearing himself away (*apospasthentas*) from his dear friends, the

---

[10] Joseph Fitzmyer, *The Gospel According to Luke X-XIV* (New York: Doubleday, 1985), 1441.

elders in Ephesus, as he departs for Jerusalem, where he will be arrested, sent to Rome, and eventually martyred. Paul will never see his friends in Ephesus again. So, when he says goodbye to them, he is described as tearing himself away from them. Like St. Paul, Jesus tears himself away (*apespasthē*) from his friends the disciples, as he prays before his arrest when he is going to be separated from them in his passion and death.

Jesus Knelt and Prostrated
(see Luke 22:4; Matthew 26:39)

Fourth, the fact that Jesus knelt (literally, "was placing his knees on the ground") is another indication of the intensity of his prayer. In no other scriptural text do we ever read about Jesus' posture in prayer. The expression *tithenai gonata* is used four other times in Luke's writings—all in contexts involving death. Stephen knelt in prayer when he was being stoned to death (see Acts 7:60). Peter knelt before raising Tabitha from the dead (see Acts 9:40). Before departing for Jerusalem where he would be arrested, Paul knelt when saying goodbye to those beloved elders in Ephesus, whom Paul knew he would not see again (see Acts 20:36). He knelt again when his disciples told him not to go up to Jerusalem where we would be arrested (see Acts 21:5). As biblical scholar Alois Stöger explains, "When they were confronted with the power of death, they all prayed kneeling down. Martyrdom can be overcome only by prayer. Jesus is the model of martyrs."[11]

Fifth, Matthew and Mark mention how Jesus also "fell on his face" during his prayer (Matthew 26:39; Mark 14:35). In the Bible, lying on the ground prostrate was a posture of supplication in prayer (see Luke 5:12; 17:16) and a reverential response before

[11] Alois Stöger, *The Gospel According to Saint Luke II*, vol. 1 (London: Burns & Oats, 1969), 109, as cited in Benedict XVI (Joseph Ratzinger), *Jesus of Nazareth: Holy Week* (New York: Doubleday, 2011), 154.

God's presence or to a supernatural experience (see Genesis 17:3, 18:2, 19:1; Judges 13:20; Daniel 8:17; Mathew 17:6). According to Benedict XVI, in this context, Jesus' falling on his face is "the prayer posture of extreme submission to the will of God, of radical self-offering to him."[12]

Each of these five details tells us something for our own lives. When we have our own Gethsemane moments—when we face trials, become distraught or experience intense sorrow in our soul—we must do what Jesus does: Turn to the Lord, withdraw to a quiet place for prayer, fall on our knees and beg God for help, prostrate at least in our hearts before the Almighty God, trust in his care for us, and humbly submit to whatever may be his will.

The stage is now set. The devil is on the move, and Jesus is getting ready for the battle. He goes to the Mount of Olives to pray. Feeling the pressure of the moment, Jesus is "greatly distraught" and "sorrowful to death" (Mark 13:33-34). He tears away from his disciples, gets on his knees, and prostrates himself. What is it that Jesus will pray that brings about such agony?

———————— **REFLECTION QUESTIONS** ————————

- *What do you think caused Jesus the most agony when he arrived in Gethsemane?*

- *What are some of the things Jesus did to face his trial—to deal with his becoming distraught and sorrowful?*

- *How might you imitate Jesus the next time you face a difficult trial—a "Gethsemane moment"?*

---

12 Benedict XVI, *Jesus of Nazareth: Holy Week*, 153.

Chapter Two

THE PRAYER OF THE AGONY

Fruit on an olive tree

"My Father, if it is possible, let this cup pass from me"
—Matthew 26:39 (NAB)

Have you ever wondered about Jesus' prayer in the garden? Is Jesus, at the last minute, having second thoughts? Is he suddenly trying to avoid the Cross? Is he wavering on his commitment to go to Calvary and "give his life as a ransom for many" (Matthew 20:28)?

Let us unpack the meaning of this prayer.

First, Jesus addresses God in a remarkably personal and intimate way. He does not just call God "Father," as he did elsewhere (see Matthew 11:25) and which was common in Old Testament Israel. He addresses God as "*My* Father" (Matthew 26:39, emphasis added). He even calls God *"Abba,"* which is an affectionate term in Hebrew and Aramaic used by a son to address his own father ("Dad") (see Mark 14:36). Some Old Testament passages refer to God as the Father (*Ab*) of his people Israel as a whole (see Deuteronomy 32:6; Psalm 103:13; Jeremiah 31:9). No Old Testament text recounts an individual addressing God with the term "Abba," which boldly expresses such intimacy and trust. Whatever the meaning of Jesus' prayer may be, his calling God "My Father" and *"Abba"* indicates that he has profound closeness and trust with his heavenly Father. In the words of biblical scholar Mary Healy, "With this term of affection, Mark accents the fact that Jesus' obedience is no mere resignation but an act of unbounded trust, commitment, and love for his Father."[13]

Second, what is the meaning of the "cup" Jesus mentions? In the Old Testament, the cup is a symbol for God's punishment poured out on the sinful people (see Isaiah 51:17, 22; Jeremiah 25:15-16; Ezekiel 23:33; Lamentations 4:21). It is used this way in the book of Revelation as well (see Revelation 14:10, 16:19). Jesus himself speaks of the "cup" as a metaphor for the suffering and death he will face as he takes on the punishment for our sins (see Matthew 20:22-23). As he is about to actually drink the cup of his suffering, Jesus is feeling the full weight of what this means for him. As Pope Benedict XVI once explained, "Jesus' fear is far more radical than the fear that everyone experiences in the face of death; it is the collision between light and darkness, between life and death itself—the critical moment in human history."[14]

Pass the Cup?

Third, we come to the puzzling petition itself: "If it is possible, let this cup pass from me" (Matthew 26:39, NAB). What does

---

13 Mary Healy, *The Gospel of Mark* (Grand Rapids, MI: Baker Academic, 2008), 292.

14 Benedict XVI, *Jesus of Nazareth: Holy Week*, 156.

Jesus mean by this? Is he really wanting to avoid the cup? Is he suddenly getting cold feet and considering backing away from his mission to die for our sins?

His prayer simply reflects the fact that Jesus is *truly human.* Since suffering and death are repulsive to human nature, the torturous death Jesus is about to endure would not be something he would look forward to. In other words, if Jesus is truly human, he would not be saying, "I can't wait to do this!" No. Suffering, crucifixion, and death are repugnant to human nature. If Jesus is truly human, he would be repulsed by the thought of what he is about to endure. His prayer, therefore, "expresses the horror that death represented for his human nature" (CCC 612).

> Jesus looks at death square in the eye and still gives a wholehearted "Yes."

But Jesus is not merely human; he is also divine. Unlike our weak, fallen wills, Jesus' human will is perfectly united to his Father's (see CCC 475). That is why he says in the same prayer, "Not as I will, but as you will" (Matthew 26:39). Though he feels aversion to death in his human nature, he also is completely willing to embrace the Cross for our salvation and fulfill his Father's plan. Jesus looks at death square in the eye—feels the full weight of what he is about to bear—and still gives a wholehearted "Yes."

Jesus' example challenges us to be more like him. When we face suffering, we often hesitate to do the right thing or shrink from God's will. We fear making sacrifices, we fear change, we fear the unknown, and we let our fear of suffering prevent us from doing what is right. Jesus, however, faces that suffering, feels the full force of it, and still freely embraces it for the sake of our salvation, completely accepting the Father's will.

Bad Tasting Medicine

The thirteenth century theologian St. Thomas Aquinas explains this prayer of Christ with the analogy of taking bad tasting medicine. An adult who is ill may know that a certain medicine has a horrible taste. He absolutely dreads consuming it, but he also realizes that it is good for him, and that he needs it to be healthy again. So, despite his strong distaste for the drug, he willingly swallows it so that he can be healed.

Similarly, Jesus, because he is fully human, knows how painful and how bad tasting the medicine of the Cross will be. His words express his natural repugnance to it: "My Father, if it is possible, let this cup pass from me" (Matthew 26:39, NAB). But because his human will is perfectly united to his Father's will, he does not waiver. He does not hesitate. In the same breath, he expresses his total commitment to take the medicine of the Cross so that humanity can be healed from the illness of sin. Thus, he concludes, "Not as I will, but as you will" (Matthew 26:39).

This analogy hits home for me. There are times I have wished my little children took their medicine the way Jesus did his in Gethsemane—peacefully and promptly swallowing it without all the fussing. But when our toddler recently needed to take some liquid medication, she kicked and screamed and kept her lips closed tightly. She did everything she could to prevent any medication from entering her mouth. When we finally were able to force a few drops in, she spit it out all over the floor, the furniture, and our clothes, making a mess everywhere.

We adult children of God sometimes do the same thing. When the Lord asks us to carry a certain cross, we do not always embrace it. When we sense we are supposed to do something difficult—accept a setback or suffering, make a change, repent of a sin, tell someone we are sorry, give up our plans and control—like Jesus, we feel the weight of what is being asked of us. We feel how hard it might be to say: "Yes." But unlike Jesus, we usually do not immediately embrace the cross. Like little children, we kick and scream and resist the bad tasting medicine even though it will bring greater healing to our souls. We tend to hesitate, procrastinate, and evade the cross that God wants us to carry. And we make a big mess of our lives and those of others in the process!

Let us be more like Jesus in the garden; let us have the disposition of total trust and total surrender. Not every desire or fear we have is a good one. Let us entrust whatever desires or fears we have, whatever opportunities or crosses that come our way, to the Father's will. Like Christ, may we always trust God's plan more than our own by saying, "Not as I will, but as you will" (Matthew 26:39).

Strengthened by an Angel

"And there appeared to him an angel from heaven, strengthening him" (Luke 22:43). Notice how the Father responds to Jesus' prayer. He does not remove the cup of suffering, but he sends an angel to strengthen Jesus.

Throughout Scripture, God sends angels to help those in distress. An angel gave Elijah food to strengthen him (see 1 Kings 19:5-8); angels guard and support the faithful (see Psalm 91:11-12). Angels especially come to strengthen those who are being persecuted or martyred. When the three young Israelites were thrown into the fiery furnace for refusing to worship an idol, an angel comes to save them (see Daniel 3:49). When the prophet Daniel is discouraged and weary, overwhelmed by the persecution the Jewish people will face, an angel touched him and strengthened him (see Daniel 10:15-19). In the non-canonical Jewish text 3 Maccabees, when some faithful Jews are about to be martyred by the Egyptians, the priest Eleazar prays and two angels descend from heaven to rescue them from death (3 Maccabees 6:18).

Luke himself draws on this motif in the Acts of the Apostles. He explains that when the Sadducees arrested the apostles, "an

angel of the Lord opened the prison doors and brought them out"
(Acts 5:19). God similarly sent an angel to Peter and Paul when
they faced persecution. An angel rescued Peter when Herod
imprisoned him (see Acts 12:7), and an angel encouraged Paul
during his treacherous voyage to Rome where he would stand
before Caesar (see Acts 27:23). Time and again, God responds
to his people's needs by sending an angel to help them. That
is what the Father does for Jesus in Gethsemane. He responds
to Jesus' prayer not by removing the cup but by providing the
strength he needs to drink it. And the same is true for us today.
St. Paul explains, "God is faithful, and he will not let you be
tempted beyond your strength" (1 Corinthians 10:13). He may
not remove the trials we face, but he will always give us the
strength we need to face them.

All this sheds light on the angel's appearance in Gethsemane,
but for Jesus, it likely brought to mind another moment when
angels came to his aid: when he was tested in the desert three
times by the devil. When that ordeal was over, "angels came and
ministered to him" (Matthew 4:11).

Think about the significance of that. There are only two times
in the Gospels when angels come to minister to Jesus: when he
was tempted by the devil at the start of his public ministry and
here at the climax of his mission when he is agonizing in the
garden. What does that tell us? If the last time angels ministered
to Christ was at his showdown with Satan, the appearance of an
angel strengthening him in the garden is another indication that
a darker force is lurking in the background. The one ultimately
working against Jesus in Gethsemane is not Judas, not the chief
priests, and not the soldiers, but Satan.

His Sweat Became Like Drops of Blood

The intensity of Jesus' ordeal in the garden is magnified in the
next verse of Luke's Gospel: "And being in an agony, he prayed

more earnestly; and his sweat became like great drops of blood falling down to the ground" (Luke 22:44).

What is the nature of Jesus' profuse sweat at this moment? Did he really sweat drops of blood? Or is this just a simile or symbol?

Some scholars point out that the Greek word for "like" (*hōs* or *hōsei*) can be understood as making a metaphorical connection. In this case, Luke's description that Jesus' sweat became "*like* drops of blood" should be understood in a figurative way. Jesus began to sweat so profusely it was as if his drops of sweat falling from his face were like drops of blood falling to the ground—not that he actually had bloody sweat.

Yet, the word "like" is used elsewhere in Luke to express a real identification. The prodigal son, for example, says to his father, "Make me like (*hōs*) one of your hired servants" (Luke 15:19). In another parable, charges were brought against a steward who was accused "as" (*hōs*) wasting his master's possessions. In these cases, the word "as" implies a real association, not just a metaphor. The prodigal son actually wants to be treated as a hired servant, and the steward was accused of really mismanaging his master's wealth. In this light, Jesus' sweat becoming like (*hōsei*) drops of blood is no mere metaphor. Jesus began to sweat so intensely that his sweat became bloody—a condition which was known in ancient times and cited in some modern medical studies as well.[15]

Runner's Agony

When the sweat imagery is linked with what Luke states next— that Jesus is in "agony"—the symbolism is even more dramatic (see Luke 22:44). This is the only time in the New Testament that the word *agōnia* is used. In Greek, *agōnia* describes a struggle for triumph in a great contest. It recalls the ordeal ancient runners

---

[15] As Brown notes, some medical studies cite the condition of *hematidrosis,* which involves "intense dilation of subcutaneous capillaries that burst into the sweat glands. The blood then clots and is carried to the surface of the skin by sweat." Brown, *The Death of the Messiah,* 1:185.

experienced when they were getting ready to begin a race. As they approached the starting line, athletes sometimes became so intense that sweat broke out all over their bodies. This moment was known as the runner's "agony."

Luke's depiction of Jesus sweating intensely like an athlete is fitting, for the New Testament uses this athletic imagery elsewhere to describe heroic perseverance in faith. Just as an athlete exercises self-control in all things to win a perishable crown—a mere wreath—so we should strive for self-control as we run after something much greater: the imperishable crown that awaits us in heaven (see 1 Corinthians 9:25-26). Similarly, Paul describes his own faith journey in athletic terms saying he has "fought the good fight" and "finished the race" as he awaits "the crown of righteousness" that will be awarded for his faithfulness (2 Timothy 4:7-8).

With this background in mind, think about how Luke's original readers may have viewed the scene of Jesus in the garden. Being in "agony" and sweating intensely, Jesus is portrayed as facing an ordeal that has a lot more at stake than any race in the ancient Greek world. Jesus is battling with the devil for the salvation of the human family. Poised at the starting line of this redemptive contest, Jesus, like a runner, sweats profusely, manifesting the intensity of the trial he is about to undergo.

──────────── **REFLECTION QUESTIONS** ────────────

- *In Gethsemane, Jesus surrenders perfectly to the Father's will when he prays, "Not as I will but as you will" (Matthew 26:39). On a scale of 1 to 10, how willing are you to surrender decisions and life situations to the Father's will?*

- *What are some of the things that keep you from entrusting your life to the Father's plan for you? Fear? Not wanting to give up control? Not being convinced God is trustworthy? Not wanting to surrender your plans to his plans?*

- *In the Bible, God says, "For I know the plans I have for you, says the Lord, plans for welfare and not for evil, to give you a future and a hope" (Jeremiah 29:11). How might this verse give you confidence to seek and do the Father's will for your life.*

Chapter Three

WATCH AND PRAY

Sanctuary in the Church of All Nations, Jerusalem,
Guiding Star Pilgrimages, LLC

"Watch and pray ... "
—Mark 14:38

Jesus didn't ask a lot. When he arrived in the garden of Gethsemane, he gave his apostles just two small tasks. He didn't tell them to fast, make a sacrifice, or do a 54-day novena. Nor did he ask them to start a program, preach the Gospel, or perform some noble community service. He didn't even call them to martyrdom right at this moment. And he certainly didn't ask them to pull out swords and defend him from the soldiers who would soon come to take him away. Rather, all Jesus wanted them to do is "watch and pray" with him (Mark 14:38).

Think about that. In his greatest moment of agony, as he was preparing to face the full brunt of his passion and death, Jesus simply wanted his apostles' hearts: their friendship, their time, their full attention, their love. He asked them to keep *watch* with him and to *pray* with him.

Are you willing to be there for Jesus, to be present to him in the garden? To give him your time and devotion? Do you love Jesus enough to take time each day to keep watch with him and pray with him? If we want to be faithful disciples, we, too, must stay awake spiritually amid our daily lives and keep watch and pray with Jesus. Let's unpack the rich biblical background to what these two commands meant originally for Peter, James, and John in Gethsemane—and what they mean for us today.

Keeping Watch

First, Jesus tells Peter, James and John to "watch" while he goes a little further from them to pray on his own (see Mark 14:34). But what is it that Jesus wants them to watch? Is he simply exhorting them to stay awake? Is he going to perform some kind of demonstration that he wants them to observe carefully? Or is Jesus telling them to keep watch in order to stay on guard against some threat?

The word for "watch" in Mark 14:34 expresses not just a one-time look (Hey, watch this!), but implies a continual vigilance— to keep watch. Moreover, the verb "watch" describes not just being physically awake—though the apostles will need help with that, too—but a *spiritual* alertness for whatever trials may come their way. It depicts the necessary spiritual vigilance the disciples need to prepare for the trials surrounding God's coming in judgment, for "you know neither the day nor the hour" (Matthew 25:13; see also Matthew 24:42).

In fact, the apostles would have been very familiar with Jesus' command to "watch" (*grēgorein*), because the last time they were all together on the Mount of Olives, Jesus emphasized that command three times. After telling the apostles to "watch and pray," Jesus had given a parable about a doorkeeper in which the master goes away leaving the servants in charge, while the doorkeeper is to keep watching. In the parable, Jesus used the verb "watch" (*grēgorein*) three times, while exhorting the apostles to stay vigilant, "for you do not know when the master of the house will come" (Mark 13:34, 35, 37).

> **Are you willing to be there for Jesus, to give him your time, attention and devotion?**

Now, on that same Mount of Olives, Jesus once again urgently admonishes his apostles to keep up that same kind of vigilance—and he again uses the same key word "watch" (*grēgorein*) three times: "remain here, and *watch*," "Could you not *watch* one hour? "and "*Watch* and pray" (Mark 14:34, 37, 38). Jesus pleads with them to be ready to face their most intense challenge in discipleship. Indeed, they are about to be tested like never before. It is as if Jesus is giving the disciples the same exhortation found in 1 Peter 5:8: "Be sober, be watchful. Your adversary the devil prowls around like a roaring lion, seeking someone to devour. Resist him, firm in your faith."

The Devil Seeking to Devour

That the devil is seeking to devour the apostles in the garden is made clear by what Jesus says next: "Watch and pray *that you may not enter into temptation*" (Mark 14:38, emphasis added). The word for temptation (*peirasmon*) brings to mind Satan tempting (*peirazein*) Jesus in the desert (see Mark 1:13). When Jesus admonishes the apostles to pray not to enter into temptation (*peirsamon*), he's not thinking primarily of smaller temptations like falling asleep during prayer. Rather, the expression recalls his own trials in the wilderness when he faced the devil's onslaught, being tempted (*peirazein*) three times to break his commitment to his heavenly Father. That's the kind of ordeal the apostles are about the face. It will be a superhuman trial, and only God can protect them (see 2 Peter 2:4-10; Revelation 3:20). That's why

Jesus exhorts them to turn to God in prayer for help. Though they cannot avoid the trial that's coming, they are to pray not to *enter into* the *peirasmos*.

This line, of course, recalls the Our Father. In the Lord's Prayer, Jesus taught us to say, "Lead us not into temptation (*peirasmos*), but deliver us from the Evil One." Notice how the temptation is not a random test, but one that comes from the devil. These petitions in the Lord's Prayer remind us that evil is not an abstract concept or some vague force in the world, but a person—the fallen angel called the devil. He is the "Evil One," the adversary who opposes all that is good.

Five Keys for Spiritual Battle

When we pray "lead us not into temptation," we are not asking God to help us avoid all trials and temptations. We cannot escape temptation in this fallen world, but we pray for God to protect us from *giving in* to those trials. As the Catechism explains, this petition basically means "do not allow us to enter into temptation" or "do not let us yield to temptation."[16]

Practically speaking, how do we do this? What can we do the next time we find ourselves tempted to anger, pride, or vanity, worrying about what others think of us, or struggling with purity, envy, fear, anxiety, or discouragement? Here are five simple things you can do right away to resist temptation.

First, remember that Jesus taught us in Gethsemane to watch and pray. Just say a quick prayer. Simply bringing God into the middle of your trials always helps. Sometimes we face such anxiety, panic, and inner turmoil that we forget to ask God for help.

Second, you can simply speak the name of Jesus, for there is power in his holy name. St. Paul told us that even the demons must immediately submit to Christ's name. "At the name of Jesus,

---

[16] CCC 2846.

every knee must bow in heaven, on earth and under the earth" (Philippians 2:10). Christians throughout the centuries have found Jesus' name to be a powerful defense against the enemy.

Third, make the Sign of the Cross. Many early Christians turned to the Sign of the Cross in moments of temptation, believing that the demons plaguing them would flee. St. Cyril of Jerusalem described the Sign of the Cross prayer as "a terror to the devils ... For when they see the Cross, they are reminded of the Crucified; they fear him who has 'smashed the heads of dragons.'"[17] The Sign of the Cross has power. It is like a spiritual sword right on your hand. Trace the cross over your body, say the words, and be confident that the demons are being driven back. Do not wait to pull it out. Use it the next time you face temptation. Use it today.

Fourth, you can also turn to your guardian angel. Jesus was strengthened by an angel in Gethsemane during his own ordeal. You have an angel by your side ready to strengthen and defend you at any moment in your trials. Do you ask your guardian angel to help you in the spiritual battles you face each day?

Finally, you can humbly acknowledge your weakness and beg God not to let you be tempted beyond your ability. God cannot help but come down to aid a humble soul crying to him for assistance. According to Pope Benedict XVI, when we pray in the Our Father "lead us not into temptation," it is as if we are saying to God, "I know that I need trials so that my nature can be purified. When you decide to send me these trials, when you give evil some room to maneuver, as you did with Job, then please remember that my strength goes only so far ... Don't set too wide the boundaries within which I may be tempted, and be close to me with your protecting hand when it becomes too much for me."[18]

---

[17] St. Cyril of Jerusalem, *Catechetical Lecture* 13, 3, as translated in Andreas Andreopoulos, *The Sign of the Cross: The Gesture, The Mystery, The History* (Brewster, MA: Paraclete, 2006).

[18] Benedict XVI, *Jesus of Nazareth,* vol. 1 (New York: Doubleday, 2007), 163.

If you ever attend a Holy Thursday Liturgy, you probably will notice how the ending is dramatically different than any other Mass.

The altar is stripped of its cloths, recalling how Jesus will be stripped of his garments on Good Friday. And there is no closing line, "The Mass is ended … ," or a closing hymn. Instead, the priest leads a procession throughout the Church or even outdoors with the Eucharist, singing hymns, and bringing the Eucharist to a side chapel. This is reminiscent of Jesus leaving the Last Supper, singing hymns (see Mark 14:26), and going from Jerusalem to the Garden of Gethsemane to pray.

On that first Holy Thursday night, Jesus told the apostles, "Watch and pray" (Mark 14:38) and "remain here, and watch" (Mark 14:34). But they fell asleep that night and could not keep vigil with him. What will you do? Whether it be your next Holy Thursday night or any ordinary day throughout the year, Jesus invites you to stay with him, and to pray with him. He is present in every tabernacle throughout the world, even until the end of time. Will you "watch and pray" with him?

—————— REFLECTION QUESTIONS ——————

- *We saw that when Jesus instructs the apostles to "watch and pray" (Mark 14:38), the word for "watch" implies not a one-time glance, but a consistent continual watching with the Lord. How well do you do in taking time each day to spend time with Jesus, to gaze upon him in prayer? What can you do to build in time to live out Jesus' command to consistently watch and pray with him?*

- *Jesus tells the apostles "pray that you may not enter into temptation" (Mark 14:38). The first step in this battle is to recognize the kinds of temptations we tend to face, such as pride, anger, gossip, discouragement, anxiety about the future, lust, sloth, or others. What are some of the main temptations you tend to face?*

- *What are some simple things you can do right away to help you resist temptation?*

Chapter Four

PROPHECY FULFILLED: FROM SHADOWS TO REALITY

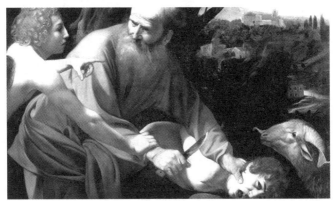

The Sacrifice of Isaac by Michelangelo Merisi da Caravaggio

"I wish the ring had never come to me."

If I spoke these words to an audience, many people would immediately recognize I was quoting a famous line in J.R.R. Tolkein's work *The Lord of the Rings*. But if you were not familiar with the story and the main character Frodo Baggins—who spoke these words when feeling overwhelmed by his perilous mission to destroy the ring of power—you would not catch the allusion I was making. You would probably be a bit confused. You might even wonder if I were having a marriage crisis and thinking about taking off my wedding ring!

Something similar happens when reading the Passion narratives. Matthew, Mark, Luke, and John are constantly making allusions to stories that have come before: the stories of the Old Testament.

But do we make the connections? Do we notice the allusions? Do we catch the fulfillment of prophecy? The more we know about those stories of old, the more we will grasp what the Gospels are telling us about Jesus. Men like Adam, Moses, and David and events like the Passover and the Exodus and institutions like the Temple and the ancient Israelite priesthood are not just parts of stories from a long time ago. They each were given to us by God to prefigure Christ in various ways, each serving as an important prophetic foreshadowing of his passion and death.

We see this particularly in the garden of Gethsemane. In this chapter, we are going to step back for a moment and focus on just three examples of how God uses events from the past to tell us something important about what his Son is doing for us in his passion. Two examples come from the Old Testament: the fall of Adam and the sacrifice of Isaac. The other comes from an event that occurred earlier in Jesus' own public ministry: his Transfiguration.

> **Through all the individual stories of the Old Testament, God has been preparing his people for this climactic night in Jerusalem.**

In the process, we'll discover that what happens to Jesus in Gethsemane does not come out of the blue. It was all anticipated by Christ himself and foreshadowed by God in the Old Testament. If you know the stories that came before, you will more fully grasp how God's plan of salvation has been at work ever since the beginning of time. What God had been doing in the lives of Adam, Abraham, Moses, and David and through the priesthood, the Temple, and the Torah all had a profound purpose. These are not individual, isolated stories about random people, institutions, and events. Rather, they all are important pieces to a much bigger puzzle. They all come together in the one overarching story of God's saving plan.

Think of it this way: God didn't give the Exodus, the Ten Commandments, the Davidic dynasty, and the many heroes of the Old Testament simply to help the ancient people of Israel. In his providence, God gave these people and events in history also to help you and me today recognize and understand his Son, Jesus Christ, and the kingdom he came to establish. Indeed, through all the individual stories of the Old Testament, God has been preparing his people for this climactic night in Jerusalem—for this very moment in the garden of Gethsemane—when Christ's passion brings the entire story of Scripture to its epic culmination.

New Adam

We've seen how Luke's Gospel portrays the agony in the garden scene as the "opportune time" when the devil tests Jesus. We've also seen how Jesus does the Father's will and his sweat becomes like drops of blood. These themes of the devil, a test, sweat, and doing God's will—all this taking place in a garden (John 18:1)— would bring to mind for the Jews in Jesus' day another similar event that took place at the beginning of time: the fall of Adam.

First, notice the parallels between Adam's trial and Christ's. Both were tested by the devil in a garden: Adam was tested in the Garden of Eden, while Jesus is tested in the garden of Gethsemane. Adam proved to be unfaithful, preferring his own will to God's will. Jesus, however, proves to be a faithful Son, saying to the Father, "Not as I will, but as you will." Adam disobeyed God and ate from the forbidden Tree of Knowledge of Good and Evil, while Jesus was obedient to his Father's will and embraced the wood of the Cross—which Christians would eventually call the new Tree of Life.

Second, Jesus took on the consequences of Adam's sin. Recall how when Adam sinned in the Garden, he became ashamed in his *nakedness* (Genesis 3:11), was expelled from *paradise* (Genesis 3:24), and was afflicted by various curses. God said to Adam:

> Cursed is the ground because of you; in toil you shall eat of it
> all the days of your life; thorns and thistles it shall bring forth
> to you ... In the sweat of your face you shall eat bread till you
> return to the ground, for out of it you were taken; you are dust,
> and to dust you shall return. (Genesis 3:17-19)

It is important to unpack the key points here. The *ground* in which Adam toiled was now cursed. His work would no longer be easy. He would have to labor in *sweat* and his work would not always bear fruit. Instead, the ground would often yield *thorns* and thistles. Adam's greatest curse, however, was *death*. He would no longer live forever, but instead, return to the ground from which he came.

Back to the Garden

Now think about how Jesus takes on these curses of Adam. Jesus *sweats* intensely in his agony in the garden as he cleaves to his Father's will (see Luke 22:44). The next day, he will be crowned with *thorns* (see Matthew 27:29), stripped of his garments (see Matthew 27:28), and nailed to the wood of the Cross. He experiences the curse of *death* and is buried in the cursed *ground* in a garden.

But Jesus' death is not the final word. From that cursed ground, Jesus will rise again on Easter and offer new life to all the sons and daughters of Adam who have been kept out of paradise ever since the Fall. This hope of the New Adam is anticipated even on Good Friday when Jesus proclaims that he is returning to paradise and will take the children of Adam with him. One of the first to enter is the repentant good thief to whom Jesus says, "Today you will be with me in *Paradise*" (Luke 23:43, emphasis added).

In sum, Jesus faces a testing by the devil in a garden like Adam did. But Jesus proves to be faithful where Adam was unfaithful. Jesus also takes on the shame and the curses of the first Adam—the nakedness, the sweat, the thorns, death, and returning to the ground—so that he can open the gates of paradise and bring the sons of Adam with him. In the words of the fourth century theologian and bishop St. Cyril of Jerusalem,

> Jesus assumes the thorns that he might cancel the doom; for this cause also was he buried in the earth, that the cursed earth might receive, instead of the curse, the blessing. In [the garden of] paradise was the fall, and in a Garden was our salvation. From the Tree came sin, and until the Tree [of the cross] sin lasted; in the evening they sought to hide themselves from the eyes of the Lord and in the evening the robber is brought by the Lord into Paradise.[19]

ADAM	JESUS
Tested in the Garden of Eden (see Genesis 3).	Tested in the Garden of Gethsemane (see Luke 22:39-46).
Preferred his own will to God's will (see Genesis 3).	Submitted to the Father's will, saying, "Not as I will, but as you will" (Matthew 26:39).
Ate from the forbidden Tree of Knowledge of Good and Evil (see Genesis 3:6).	Nailed to the "tree" of the cross (see Acts 5:30).
Curse of sweat (see Genesis 3:19).	Sweat drops like blood (see Luke 22:44).
Curse of thorns (see Genesis 3:18).	Crown of thorns (see Mathew 27:29).
Curse of death (see Genesis 3:19).	Jesus dies (see Luke 23:46).
Ground cursed (see Genesis 3:17).	Buried in the ground in a garden tomb (see John 19:41).
Nakedness exposed (see Genesis 3:11).	Stripped of his garments (see Matthew 27:28).
Expelled from Paradise (see Genesis 3:24).	Reopened paradise and took the "good thief" with him (see Luke 23:42-43).

---

[19] St. Cyril of Jerusalem, P.G. 33, 796A-B. As translated in Jean Danielou, *From Shadows to Reality* (London: Burns & Oates, 1960), 42.

The Sacrifice of Isaac

A second theme that emerges in the garden of Gethsemane is how Matthew's Gospel portrays Jesus in ways that recall the sacrifice of Isaac, the son of Abraham. In fact, the story of the sacrifice of Isaac is one of the most important Old Testament foreshadowings of Jesus' own sacrifice on Calvary. To appreciate this beautiful prophetic prefiguring, walk with me now as we consider how the details of that story relate to Jesus' passion and death.

The drama begins with God telling Abraham: "Take your son, your only begotten son Isaac, whom you love, and go to the land of Moriah, and offer him there as a burnt offering upon one of the mountains of which I shall tell you" (Genesis 22:2). Abraham obeys the Lord, cuts the wood for the sacrifice, saddles his donkey, and begins this journey with his son to Moriah. As they ascend the mountain, Isaac carries the wood for the sacrifice on his shoulders.

When they arrive at the top, Abraham gets the altar ready, binds Isaac, and lays his son on the altar of wood. Just as he is about to slay his son, God sends an angel to stop him, saying "Abraham, Abraham! ... Do not lay your hand on the lad or do anything to him; for now I know that you fear God, seeing you have not withheld your son, your only son, from me" (Genesis 22:11-12). God then promises Abraham that his family will be the instrument he uses to bring blessing to the rest of the world. "Because you have done this, and have not withheld your son, your only son, I will indeed bless you, and I will multiply your descendants ... and by your descendants shall all the nations of the earth bless themselves" (Genesis 22:16-18).

The particulars of this story prefigure what will happen on this same mountain a couple thousand years later when Jesus dies on the Cross. For the sacred location where Isaac was to be sacrificed—Mount Moriah—later came to be associated with Jerusalem (see 2 Chronicles 3:1; Psalm 76:1-3). Therefore, just as

God instructed Abraham to "take your only son ... whom you love" to be offered as a sacrifice on Mount Moriah, so God the Father takes his only beloved Son, Jesus Christ, to be offered on the mountain of Jerusalem. Similarly, just as Isaac went up Moriah on a donkey, so Jesus entered Jerusalem on a donkey. And just as Isaac carried the wood for the sacrifice up Moriah, so Jesus carries the wood of the Cross up to Calvary. Isaac was to be offered as a burnt offering—which often was an offering for sin— so Jesus offers himself as the sacrifice for the sins of all humanity.

Most profound is that in the ancient Jewish and early Christian tradition, Isaac was not a passive victim, but someone who willingly cooperated with the sacrifice. Think about it. Isaac likely was at least in his teens at the time. The Bible makes clear he was at least old enough to carry the wood up the mountain and mature enough to understand the intricacies for the specific type of sacrifice being offered (see Genesis 22:7). If he could do that, he was likely wise enough to realize what was happening and strong enough either to run away or resist his elderly father who was over one hundred years old at the time. Hence, it is no surprise that several ancient Jewish rabbis and Christian Church Fathers assumed Isaac was a voluntary victim. He freely chose to submit to God's command and go through with the sacrifice, even if this meant his own death.

ISAAC	JESUS
Beloved son (see Genesis 22:2).	"Beloved Son" (Mark 1:11).
To be sacrificed as a burnt offering (an offering for sin) (see Genesis 22:3).	Sacrificed for the sins of the world (see John 1:29).
To be sacrificed on Mount Moriah, which later became associated with Jerusalem (see Genesis 22:2).	Sacrificed on Golgotha, just outside Jerusalem (see Matthew 27:33).

ISAAC	**JESUS**
Isaac carried the wood for the sacrifice on the way up the mountain (see Genesis 22:6).	Jesus carried the wood of the Cross on the way to Golgotha (see John 19:17).
Isaac was bound and laid on the wood for the sacrifice (see Genesis 22:9).	Jesus was nailed to the Cross, the wood for the sacrifice (see Acts 5:30).
Isaac was a voluntary victim (see Genesis 22).	Jesus was a voluntary victim (see John 10:18).
Isaac's willingness to be sacrificed led to the promise for a worldwide blessing coming through Abraham's family (see Genesis 22:16-18).	Jesus' willingness to be sacrificed brought the promised blessing to the whole world (see Mark 16:15-16).

A New Isaac in Gethsemane

Matthew gives special attention to Jesus being a new Isaac, especially in his accounts of what happened in Gethsemane. He makes four points that underscore how he wants us to view these scenes in light of the sacrifice of Isaac.

First, when Jesus arrives at the garden, he tells the apostles, "Sit here while I go yonder and pray." This echoes what Abraham said to his men at Mount Moriah when he was taking Isaac up for the sacrifice: "Stay here with the ass; I and the lad will go yonder and worship" (see Matthew 26:36; Genesis 22:5).

Second, when Matthew describes how the crowds arrive to arrest Jesus "with swords (*machairōn*) and clubs (*zulōn*)," he uses the same two Greek words the Septuagint uses to describe the knife (*machaira* in Genesis 22:6, 10) and wood (*zula* in Genesis 22:3, 6, 7, 9) Abraham needed for the sacrifice of Isaac.

Third, just as Peter "stretched out his hand and drew his sword," so Abraham "put forth his hand, and took the knife"

(Matthew 26:51; Genesis 22:10). And fourth, just as the crowd "laid hands" on Christ to arrest him, so the angel says to Abraham, "Do not lay your hands on the boy" (Matthew 26:50; Genesis 22:12).[20]

ISAAC ON MOUNT MORIAH (GENESIS 22)	JESUS ON MOUNT OF OLIVES (MATTHEW 26)
"Stay here ... I and the lad will go yonder and worship" (Genesis 22:5).	"Sit here, while I go over there and pray" (Matthew 26:36).
"knife (*machaira*) and wood (*zula*)" (Genesis 22:6).	"Swords (*machairōn*) and clubs (*zulōn*)" (Matthew 26:47).
Abraham "put forth his hand, and took the knife" (Genesis 22:10).	Peter "stretched out his hand and drew his sword" (Matthew 26:51).
"Do not lay your hands on the boy" (Genesis 22:12).	The crowd "laid hands" on Christ (Matthew 26:50).

With all these parallels, it is clear that Matthew wants us to understand Jesus' arrest in the garden in light of the sacrifice of Isaac on Mount Moriah.

The main point to take away is that in the garden of Gethsemane, at the start of Christ's passion, Jesus is depicted in ways that recall Isaac's sacrifice: the mention of swords and clubs, Jesus' words "Sit here, while I go yonder and pray," and the mention that Peter "stretched out his hand and drew his sword." How fitting it is, at this precise moment, for Matthew to frame our view of Christ's passion with this most crucial moment in Isaac's life. Most of all, it subtly reminds us that, like Isaac, Jesus is not a passive victim. He is not being carried away by the temple police against his will. Like Isaac, Jesus willingly lays down his life. "I lay

---

[20] Leroy Huizenga, *The New Isaac: Tradition and Intertextuality in the Gospel of Matthew* (Leiden, Netherlands: Brill, 2002), 250-252.

down my life, that I may take it again. No one takes it from me, but I lay it down of my own accord" (John 10:17-18).

In our journey through Christ's passion, we will see many other fascinating parallels between Jesus and various Old Testament figures: Jesus and the Passover Lamb, Jesus and David, Jesus and the High Priest, and Jesus and the Suffering Servant of Isaiah's prophecies. However, you do not always have to go back to the Old Testament to find profound biblical connections to Christ's passion. Some are rooted in events earlier in Jesus' own life. Let us step back now and consider a beautiful parallel between Jesus' agony in the garden and a key turning point in Jesus' public ministry: the Transfiguration.

Why Peter, James, and John?

"And he took with him Peter, James and John ..."(Mark 14:33)

Why did Jesus take Peter, James, and John with him? These three had been singled out before. At the Transfiguration, Jesus called Peter, James, and John to witness his glory revealed on the high mountain (see Mark 9:2-8). It is now on another mountain—the Mount of Olives—at the climax of his ministry in Jerusalem, that Jesus invites them to be witnesses to his agony.

The parallels between these two scenes are striking. At the Transfiguration, Jesus "took (*paralambanein*) with him Peter, James and John" up a mountain set apart (Mark 9:2). Similarly, in Gethsemane, Jesus "took (*paralambanein*) with him Peter, James and John" as he prays on the Mount of Olives in his agony (Mark 14:33).

At the transfiguration, God calls Jesus his "beloved son." In the garden, Jesus intimately calls God "Abba, Father" (Mark 9:7, 14:36). And just as Peter "did not know what to say" when he saw Christ transfigured before him, so Peter and the other disciples "did not know what to answer him" when Jesus found them sleeping in the garden (Mark 9:6, 14:40). At the Transfiguration, the apostles *fell on their faces* when they heard the Heavenly Father's voice. In the garden, Jesus himself *fell on his face* in his prayer to his heavenly Father (see Matthew 17:6, 26:39).

Moreover, Matthew's Gospel uses a certain expression that marks a significant turning point in both scenes. It is the words, "while he was still speaking." At the Transfiguration, the phrase introduces the Father's affirmation of Christ's true identity: While Peter "*was still speaking*, a cloud overshadowed him, and a heavenly voice declared, 'This is my beloved Son, in whom I am well pleased. Listen to him'" (Matthew 17:5, emphasis added). In Gethsemane, the phrase transitions to the betrayal, in which Judas rejects Jesus as God's beloved Son, "While Jesus *was still speaking*, Judas came to betray him" (Matthew 26:47, emphasis added).

Finally, the word "rise" signals the end of both scenes. Jesus concludes the Transfiguration scene telling the apostles to "*rise*, and have no fear" (Matthew 17:7, emphasis added) just as he concludes the agony in the garden telling them, "*Rise*, let us be going; see, my betrayer is at hand" (Matthew 26:46, emphasis added).

TRANSFIGURATION	AGONY IN THE GARDEN
On "a high mountain" (Mark 9:2).	On "the Mount of Olives" (Mark 14:26).
"Jesus took with him Peter, James and John" (Mark 9:2).	Jesus "took with him Peter, James and John" (Mark 14:33).
The disciples "fell on their faces" (Matthew 17:6).	Jesus "fell on his face" (Matthew 26:39).
Peter addresses Jesus (see Matthew 17:4).	Jesus addresses Peter (Matthew 26:40).

TRANSFIGURATION

Peter "did not know what to say" (Mark 9:6).

The Father calls Jesus "my beloved Son" (Mark 9:7).

While he was still speaking (*eti auto lalountos*), a bright cloud overshadowed him (see Matthew 17:5).

"Rise (*egerthēte*) and have no fear" (Matthew 17:7).

AGONY IN THE GARDEN

Peter and other disciples "did not know what to answer him" (Mark 14:40).

Jesus calls God "Abba, Father" (Mark 14:36).

While he was still speaking (*eti auto lalountos*), Judas came (see Matthew 26:47).

"Rise (*egerthēte*) let us be going; see, my betrayer is at hand" (Matthew 26:46).

What is the point of all these connections? At the Transfiguration, Jesus took Peter, James, and John up a mountain to prepare them for the difficult trials they would face in Jerusalem. He knew they would soon be tested like never before—seeing Jesus betrayed, arrested, beaten, humiliated, and crucified. So, he allowed these three apostles to see his countenance changed and his face shining like the sun at the Transfiguration (see Luke 9:29; Matthew 17:2), for they will be near him when the sweat of his face becomes like drops of blood falling to the ground in his agony in the garden (see Luke 22:42). Jesus gave them a glimpse of his glory in the Transfiguration, so that when they see him in his agony in the garden, they might remain confident that he still really is the glorified Son of God.

The Byzantine Catholic liturgy expresses this point in a prayer for the Feast of the Transfiguration: "You were transfigured on the mountain, and your disciples, as much as they were capable of it, beheld your glory, O Christ our God, so that when they should see you crucified they would understand that your Passion was voluntary, and proclaim to the world that you truly are the splendor of the Father."[21]

─────────── **REFLECTION QUESTIONS** ───────────

- *Before reading this chapter, what were your impressions of the Old Testament? How relevant did you think it was for our Christian Faith today?*

- *What insights from this chapter have given you a deeper appreciation for the Old Testament?*

- *Peter, James, and John were given a joyful glimpse of Christ's glory—a "mountain top" experience—at the Transfiguration to prepare them for the suffering they would face as Christ's passion began in the garden of Gethsemane. Has God ever given you certain "mountain top" experiences, such as a retreat or conference that reenergized your faith, the feeling of closeness to him in prayer, or the blessing of fellowship with other Christians? Looking back, how might those blessings have helped you when you faced difficult trials later in life?*

---

[21] Byzantine Liturgy, Feast of the Transfirguration, *Kontakion.* As cited in CCC 555.

Chapter Five

THE ARREST

Judas Betrays Jesus With a Kiss
(Fresco in the Collegiata of San Gimignana, Italy)

Picture the scene: A crowd of armed men approaching at night, carrying torches, lanterns, swords, and clubs. It is a band of soldiers, police, and captains, seeking to capture a criminal by surprise. A paid spy leads them to his hiding place. There is a bit of resistance. A sword is drawn. There is a blow to the head and an ear cut off. Still, the band of soldiers successfully seizes the criminal, binds him, and leads him away to face trial, while the members of his gang flee for their lives.

One might expect such a scenario for the capture of a notorious outlaw. But in the Gospel accounts of Jesus' arrest, these details underscore how determined the Jewish leaders were to bring Jesus to his end. They took every measure to ensure that they apprehended him this night.

They had already paid Judas, "one of the Twelve," to betray Jesus. Judas knew the garden on the Mount of Olives where

Jesus often met with his disciples (see John 18:2), and he could lead them there to arrest him quietly, away from the daytime crowds in the city (see Luke 22:6).

Moreover, the Jewish leaders in Jerusalem do not send a small delegation, but "a great crowd with swords and clubs" (Matthew 26:47). Among those present, the Gospels mention a wide range of people: some of the "chief priests and elders" (Luke 22:52); the temple police (*hypēretai*) (see John 18:3); and the "officers" who oversee them (*stratēgoi*) (see Luke 22:52);[22] as well as "a band of [Roman] soldiers" (John 18:3). In fact, John mentions a commander (*chiliarchos*) and his cohort (*speiran*), which is a technical military term for a specific number of Roman soldiers (see John 18:3,12). With Roman authorities on heightened watch during the Passover feast, perhaps the chief priests were able to secure a large dispatch of Roman troops to accompany their men and ensure a peaceful arrest.[23]

Every precaution had been made: the element of surprise, lanterns to prevent anyone from easily fleeing into the dark corners of the olive grove, weapons, clubs, and swords in case there is forceful resistance, and the large number of Jewish police and Roman troops.

Jesus, however, is not caught off guard. He is completely aware of what is unfolding. Even before the crowd arrives, he tells the apostles, "Rise, let us be going; see, my betrayer is at hand" (Mark 14:42).

---

[22] Acts 5:22-26 distinguishes the temple police (*hypēretai*) from the officer overseeing them (*stratēgoi*). Both seem to be present in the arrest scene (Luke 22:52; John 18:3). Since Roman soldiers were not permitted in the Temple, the Jewish leaders in Jerusalem had their own temple guard. See Joel Green, *The Gospel of Luke* (Grand Rapids, MI: Eerdmans, 1997), 754.

[23] Pilate may have been willing to provide the soldiers "perhaps because he feared the danger of another insurrection (cf. Mk 15:7; Lk 23:19)." Brown, *The Gospel According to John XII-XXI*, 808. Indeed, there is precedent for Roman authorities sending a large amount of soldiers for a minor mission. They used 200 soldiers with 70 horsemen and 200 spearsmen to accompany Paul from Jerusalem to Caesarea (Acts 23:23). Ben Witherington, *John's Wisdom* (Louisville: Westminster John Knox Press, 1995), 285.

Judas and the Kiss

Before arriving with the arrest party to Gethsemane, Judas had given them a sign that would help identify Jesus: "The one I shall kiss is the man; seize him and lead him away safely" (Mark 14:44; see also Matthew 26:48). Why would such a sign be needed? Was not Jesus a recognized public figure? Perhaps his face was not as well-known to some in the band descending on the garden. Maybe it was too dark to see well.

Judas using the sign of *shalom* to betray Christ recalls a few passages from the Jewish Scriptures: the deceitful kiss a general named Joab gave to Amasa to trick him and kill him in the process (see 2 Samuel 20:9), as well as the cunning kiss Jacob gave his father Isaac when veiling his true identity to steal his older brother's blessing (see Genesis 27:27). It also brings to mind the admonition in Proverbs 27:6 to distrust the kisses of an enemy.

Still, no matter how deceitful Judas' kiss was, Jesus speaks tenderly to him, using two expressions that represent the last words Jesus says to Judas in Scripture. First, he calls Judas a friend, saying "Friend, why are you here?"(Matthew 26:50). The word "friend" heightens the level of betrayal taking place. This was no ordinary follower or coworker who betrayed Jesus. This was a disciple in the inner circle, "one of the twelve"(Matthew 26:47), someone whom Jesus considered a "friend." The tragedy of this betrayal recalls Sirach 37:2, a passage we have already seen in the background of Jesus' agony in the garden: "Is it not a sorrow to the death when your friend is turned enemy?"

Second, Jesus says to him, "Judas, would you betray the Son of Man with a kiss?" (Luke 22:48). The kiss was supposed to be a sign of someone being sincerely open to Jesus and his message (see Luke 7:38, 45), so it is not surprising that Jesus interrupts Judas' attempt to kiss him with this challenge. Yet notice how Jesus addresses Judas intimately, by his personal name. Yes, we have seen how Satan had entered into Judas (see Luke 22:3). And yes, Judas is an evil traitor and indispensable agent for the Jewish leaders' plot against Jesus. But he still remains a human person—a man with a face and a name. He still remains someone particularly dear to Jesus as one of the twelve. He is "friend," and Jesus addresses him personally, by name—"Judas"—as if to give one last appeal that might touch his heart and inspire him to turn away from treachery: "*Judas*, would you betray the Son of man with a kiss?" (Luke 22:48, emphasis added).

Think of how kind Jesus was to Judas, calling him by name and referring to him as "friend." All Judas needed to do was turn to Jesus and repent—to say he was sorry and stop his evil deed. If that is how gentle and merciful Christ was with Judas the betrayer, imagine how he looks at us in the midst of our weakness. Even when we sin, Jesus still reaches out to us like he did Judas. He calls us by name and wants to be our friend. Will we turn to him and his mercy? Or will we turn away like Judas did?

Jesus' Power Unleashed

Though Jesus is surrounded by a large crowd of police and soldiers coming to arrest him, notice he is actually the one in charge. He is the one who takes the initiative. Jesus even comes forward and asks, "Whom do you seek?" (John 18:4). Those are not the words of a fugitive on the run or a passive victim being taken away against his will. This is the Jesus who said, "I lay down my life, that I may take it again. No one takes it from me, but I lay it down of my own accord" (John 10:17-18). He is the Lord, the one ultimately in control of the events unfolding before him.

Consider how Jesus dramatically unveils, for a quick instant, his total power over all who are present. When the people answer that they are looking for "Jesus of Nazareth," he responds, "I am" (*egō eimi*) (John 18:5). The expression can mean simply "I am he," but In John's Gospel, it carries so much more weight. For the term also can recall the divine name revealed to Moses at the burning bush (see Exodus 3:14). Indeed, in John 8:58, Jesus uses *egō eimi* in this way to point to his divine identity, and he repeats the expression here in the garden three times (see John 18:5, 6, 8). The act of Jesus revealing his divine identity is so powerful that it makes the crowd *draw back* and *fall* to the ground (see John 18:6).

> A glimpse of Christ's divine power is unleashed for a split second here in Gethsemane.

Just picture that moment. Jesus says, "I am," and Judas, the soldiers, and temple guards all draw back a few steps in awe and are floored! A glimpse of Christ's divine power is unleashed for a split second here in Gethsemane.

The specific image of the arresting party being "turned back" recalls the suffering righteous man in the psalms who says his enemies will be "*turned back* in the day when I shall call upon you" (Psalm 56:9, emphasis added) and prays that those who plot evil against him "be turned back and confounded" (Psalm 35:4).

Falling down is a reaction to divine revelation (see Daniel 2:46, 8:18; Revelation 1:17). With the crowd backing up and falling down at the revelation of his divine identity, Jesus demonstrates how powerless the Jewish temple guard and Roman soldiers really are in his presence. The scene might even recall a Jewish tradition about the power of the divine name. According to a Hellenistic Jewish writer from before the time of John's Gospel, when Moses spoke the name of God to Pharaoh, Pharaoh fell to the ground, unable to speak until raised by Moses.[24]

With his enemies drawing back and falling down at his words, Jesus clearly shows his power over those who were coming to

---

[24] Artapanus in Eusebius *Praep. Ev.* 9.27.24-26 (OTP 2:901). As cited in Craig Keener, *The Gospel of John*, vol. 2 (Grand Rapids, MI: Baker Academic, 2010), n. 124.

capture him—the Jewish temple guard and the Roman soldiers. These are representatives of the same two authorities from Jerusalem and Rome who lead Jesus to his death. Though they come with clubs, swords, lanterns, and large numbers, they are confounded by their encounter with him and are completely neutralized. They certainly do not look like the ones in charge. It is Jesus who stands out as the true leader in this scene, and he has to take over to keep the plot moving.[25] Instead of being forcefully taken away against his will, Jesus basically gives his enemies permission to arrest him.

Peter, the Sword, and Malchus

Though the Gospels make clear that Jesus is in charge of the situation, the apostles do not get it. They see the armed men ready to take Jesus captive, panic, and ask, "Lord, shall we strike with the sword?" (Luke 22:49). Peter even takes matters into his own hands. He draws his sword and cuts off the right ear of the high priest's servant, a man named Malchus (John 18:10).

The apostles fail to grasp who is really presiding over these events in the garden. They see only with human eyes. They do not see that *Jesus* is the one in charge and is allowing himself to be taken away to fulfill his Father's plan. Jesus has to spell it out for them: "Put your sword back in its place ... Do you think that I cannot appeal to my Father, and he will at once send me more than twelve legions of angels? But how then should the scriptures be fulfilled, that it must be so?" (Matthew 26:53). Jesus touched Malchus' ear and healed him, just as he healed many during his public ministry. Jesus, therefore, exemplifies his own teaching to love one's enemy and do good deeds for one's foes (see Luke 6:27-36, 22:51).

---

25 Rodney Whitacre, *John* (Downers Grove, IL: InterVarsity Press, 1999), 427.

Fleeing Apostles

Though Jesus says in the garden that "twelve legions of angels" could appear in an instant to defend him, his own twelve apostles scatter at the moment of his arrest. Mark notes that the disciples "left" (*aphienai*) Jesus and fled. Here, Mark uses a key word in his Gospel about discipleship—the word "left"—but ironically in a way that points to them *turning back* on their discipleship.

Near the start of Mark's Gospel, the word "left" was used to describe the faithfulness of the original disciples in answering the call to follow the Lord. When Jesus called Peter and Andrew along the shores of the Sea of Galilee, they "left" (*aphienai*) their nets and followed him (see Mark 1:18). When Jesus called James and John, they both "left" (*aphienai*) their father in the boat with the hired servants and followed him. But now, at this most critical moment, all the disciples are described as having "left" (*aphienai*) Jesus and fleeing. They are turning away from their lives as disciples.

In fact, Mark actually stops calling them disciples in the arrest scene. The disciple who cuts off the ear of the high priest's servant is simply called by Mark "one of those who stood by" (Mark 14:47). In other words, this individual who throughout Mark's Gospel had been a part of a group known as "the disciples" is now relegated to a group Mark merely describes as being "those who stood by." They are no longer faithfully following Jesus. They are just standing around. Mark will not even refer to them as "the disciples" again until after the Resurrection.

The Prophecy of the Naked Man

Now we come to what is one of the strangest vignettes in the Passion narratives: the story of the naked man in Gethsemane who runs away: "And a young man followed him, with nothing but a linen cloth about his body; and they seized him, but he left the linen cloth and ran away naked" (Mark 14:51-52).

Why do we need to know this? Is not this "TMI"—too much information? Why is there someone walking around in the garden with only a linen cloth around his body? And why do we need to know he left it behind to run away naked? Mark could tell us any number of things at this moment. Where did the disciples go? What was Judas thinking at this moment? Did Mary know what was happening to her Son on this night? But a random naked man running away seems to be the most bizarre thing Mark could focus on. While the description might recall for me in my household a small child after bath time leaving a towel behind and racing through the halls to find pajamas, for years I puzzled about the significance of such a scene for understanding Christ's passion in Scripture.

Yet, there is important symbolism in this scene. On a basic level, the young man represents the failure of the larger group of disciples that night. Mark notes how the crowd "seized him" just as they "seized" Jesus (see Mark 14:46, 51). And that is an important subtle point. The young man, at least initially, experiences what Jesus does. At least for a slight moment, he shares in Jesus' passion. He is seized, along with Jesus, by his enemies.

His sharing in Christ's passion, however, is short-lived. Instead of following Jesus further along the path to the Cross, he takes the way of the other failed disciples. Mark tells how the young man "left" the linen cloth and fled (*ephygon*)–the same word he used to describe how the other disciples had abandoned Jesus and fled (*ephygon*) (see Mark 14:50). And the fact that he leaves his garment behind to flee from Jesus is even more condemning. Earlier in the Gospel of Mark, Peter extols the ideals of discipleship, saying to Jesus: "We have *left all things* and have followed you" (Mark 10:28, emphasis added). Indeed, discipleship entails leaving all things to follow the Lord. This young man, however, does just the opposite. He has left all things—literally, his last possession—not to *follow* Christ, but to *run away from* him! That is, in part, why one New Testament scholar describes this young man's attempt to follow Jesus as "a miserable failure": "For when seized as Jesus had been, he is so anxious to get away that he leaves in the hands of his captors the only clothes he wears and chooses the utter disgrace of fleeing naked—an even more desperate flight than that of the other apostles."[26]

Finally, the scene of the naked man running away also may signal that prophecy is coming to fulfillment and God's judgment is coming to Israel. The prophet Amos foretold how the nation would one day be punished, in part, because "they sell the righteous for silver" (Amos 2:6). When God's judgment comes, Amos says, "He who is stout of heart among the mighty shall flee away naked in that day" (Amos 2:16). By revealing that on the night of the Last Supper, Jesus is *sold for thirty pieces of silver* (Matthew 26:15), and a disciple who should have been faithful and strong hearted, instead *ran away naked* (see Mark 14:52), the Gospels may be pointing to how the Amos 2 prophecy about God's judgment is coming to fulfillment.

Jesus is left by his disciples and taken away to Caiaphas' house. But not all disciples abandon Jesus completely. Two of those disciples—Peter and John—will re-emerge. We will encounter them again in the next scenes as they draw near to the high priest's house to see what happens next.

---

[26] Brown, *Death of the Messiah*, 1:303.

─────────── **REFLECTION QUESTIONS** ───────────

- *Judas betrayed Jesus with a kiss, which is a sign of friendship. He communicated one thing (friendship) but meant another (betrayal). Are you sincere in all your words? Or do you sometimes say things you don't really mean or are not true because you want to fit in with your peers, leave a good impression with your boss, cover up a failure with a colleague, exaggerate a hurt with your spouse, or manipulate others to get them to do what you want? What can you do to speak more sincerely and honestly?*

- *In their fear, the apostles all fled from Jesus. In what ways might fear keep you from faithfully following Jesus? For example: being afraid to remain committed to prayer when you are busy with life and worried you can't get everything done; being afraid to stand up for your faith when others might ridicule you; or being afraid to do something you know God wants you to do because you don't want to give up something or are afraid of how things will turn out.*

- *What are some of your deepest fears? Are they rational? Does God want you to be so influenced by those fears? Imagine what you could do for God, for your parish, or for your family and friends if you were not controlled by fear.*

Chapter Six

THE HIGH PRIEST
STOOD UP

Christ Before Caiaphas by Giotto c. 1305

According to John's Gospel, Jesus is first brought from Gethsemane to a preliminary interrogation led by a man named Annas, called the "high priest" (John 18:22).

At this, readers familiar with the Passion story might have questions. Was not the high priest who condemned Christ to death named Caiaphas? Who is this Annas? What is he doing questioning Jesus?

Annas was probably the most powerful Jewish leader at this time. He reigned as high priest from AD 6 to 15 and remained influential for much of the first century through his five sons, a son-in-law, and a grandson who also held this office. Annas was thus the head of a dynasty of high priests for over fifty years, which is probably why John's Gospel refers to him as "high priest" several times (see John 18:15-16, 19, 22), even though

John makes it explicit that his son-in-law Caiaphas was the one formally holding that office at the time of Jesus' trial (see John 18:13, 24). Though he no longer held the official position of high priest, Annas continued to wield a high level of authority and respect and would have been considered the power behind the authority of Caiaphas.

The house of Annas was known for greed, wealth, and power. And Christians suffered under their rule. Jesus, Stephen the first martyr, and James the brother of the Lord were all executed under priests from the house of Annas. John's Gospel tells us that it is to Annas himself that Jesus is taken first for questioning. This should not be considered the more formal gathering of the Sanhedrin—the council of Jerusalem leaders—that the Synoptic Gospels report. Caiaphas, as reigning high priest, would preside over that grand jury. The meeting with Annas is simply a pre-trial, late-night investigation, probably with the aim of getting information that could be used against Jesus when he goes before the Sanhedrin.

Light and Darkness

Annas' interrogation of Jesus zooms in on two matters that are troubling to the Jewish leaders: Jesus' disciples and his teachings (see John 18:19).

The question about Jesus' *disciples* may have significant political implications. The house of Annas had already expressed concern about the growing number of disciples becoming a threat to the Romans and something that might trigger a violent response (see John 12:50). The chief priests and Pharisees recently said, "If we let him go on thus, everyone will believe in him, and the Romans will come and destroy both our holy place and our nation." In response, Caiaphas pushed for a plan to have Jesus eliminated. "It is expedient for you that one man should die for the people, and that the whole nation should not perish" (John 12:50).

The question about Jesus' *teachings* is also a serious concern. In John's Gospel, Jesus had already gotten into trouble with the Jewish leaders in Jerusalem over his teaching, specifically his teaching about himself. He called God his own Father, making himself equal to God. It was then that they began to plot to kill him (see John 5:18). He also was accused of blasphemy when he said, "I and the Father are one" (John 10:30-33). Later, on Good Friday, the Jews will make clear that according to their law, Jesus must die "because he has made himself the Son of God" (John 19:7).

In response to Annas' questions about his teaching, Jesus has nothing to hide. He points out how he has taught openly in the synagogues and in the Temple. "Why do you ask me? Ask those who have heard me, what I said to them" (John 18:21). Jesus appealing to the public nature of his teaching stands in contrast to the secretive behavior of the Jewish leaders who failed on multiple occasions to arrest him in public as he was well-liked by the people (see John 7:26-32, 44-46, 8:20, 59). Unlike Jesus who brings his teaching to the public in the open light, Annas, Caiaphas, and the chief priests maneuver in the dark. They scheme behind the scenes and resort to bribing Judas to betray Jesus so that they can arrest him on the Mount of Olives at night, away from the large crowds that pack the city during the day (see Luke 22:6).[27]

At Christ's answer, one of the temple police slaps Jesus, saying, "Is that how you answer the high priest?" (John 18:22). Jesus does not back down. He demands justification for the slap. If his words are to be viewed as speaking sinfully to the high priest— as in Exodus 22:28 where one is commanded *not to curse a ruler of your people*—then the officer must provide testimony for that accusation. But if Jesus is speaking rightly, then the officer stands condemned of his action.

Notice how Jesus is still the one in charge. Even though he is appearing before Annas for questioning, Jesus is the one

---

[27] Craig Keener, *The Gospel of John*, 1094.

doing the questioning now. He puts his accusers on trial, making them provide a defense and testimony. No testimony is given. The challenge is ignored, and Annas sends Jesus to Caiaphas the high priest (see John 18:24).

What Is the Sanhedrin?

The Sanhedrin was the highest authority for the Jews in the New Testament period.[28] The high priest presided over this council, which consisted of seventy other members—chief priests, who were the priests in Jerusalem in charge of the Temple, and various scribes and elders. According to Jewish tradition, the number in the Sanhedrin was based on the seventy elders that Moses appointed in Numbers 11:16.

In Jesus' time, the Sanhedrin was given significant authority from the Roman governor. It functioned as a governing body and final court of appeals for the Jewish people in legal and religious matters. Based in Jerusalem and holding sessions near or within the Temple area, the Sanhedrin's primary jurisdiction was in Judea, but would send instructions to Jewish communities abroad as well.

After his initial interrogation with Annas, Jesus is brought to the house of the reigning high priest, Caiaphas, where the Sanhedrin will convene. This is where the chief priests and elders of the people recently had gathered to plot how to arrest Jesus in stealth and bring him to his death (see Matthew 26:3-5). The first part of their plan has been successfully accomplished. Jesus was quietly apprehended on the Mount of Olives. Now they begin the process of completing their plot to condemn Jesus to death.

False Testimony

Mark notes how the Sanhedrin "*sought* testimony against Jesus to put him to death" (Mark 14:55, emphasis added). This little word

---

[28] The word *synedrion* in Greek is typically translated "council."

"sought" (*ezētoun*) is charged with great meaning in Mark's Gospel, especially as Jesus nears the last days of his life. The term is often associated with the Jewish leaders conspiring against Jesus.[29] They *sought* to destroy him (see Mark 11:18). They *sought* to seize him (see Mark 12:12). They *sought* in stealth to seize and kill him (see Mark 14:1). Judas *sought* an opportunity to betray him (see Mark 14:11). Now they *sought* testimony against Jesus to bring him to death (see Mark 14:55). This is not going to be a fair trial investigating whether Jesus is innocent or guilty. Their minds are already made up. It is just a matter of justifying the conclusion they have already reached by seeking testimony to confirm it.

Moreover, notice the irony regarding the type of testimony they seek. According to Matthew's Gospel, "The whole council sought *false* testimony against Jesus" (Matthew 26:59, emphasis added). In other words, the Sanhedrin is looking for the kind of testimony—namely, *false* testimony—that violates the Ten Commandments. The Law specifically prohibits giving false testimony. "You shall not bear false witness against your neighbor" (Exodus 20:16; see also Deuteronomy 5:20). So Christ's hearing before the Sanhedrin is, at the root, based on the violation of God's Law.

> Jesus is the one doing the questioning now. He puts his accusers on trial.

That is not all. Even with the gathering of false testimonies, the statements made against Jesus do not agree. According to the Law, a single witness cannot be used as evidence against an accused man. Two or more agreeing testimonies must be given for the witness to be deemed credible (see Deuteronomy 19:15). The Sanhedrin's problem is not simply finding enough false witnesses. There were "many" of those who came forward (see Mark 14:56). The problem is that the many false testimonies

---

[29] Francis J. Maloney, *The Gospel of Mark* (Grand Rapids, MI: Baker Academic, 2002), 301-302.

themselves do not agree (see Mark 14:56). In other words, Caiaphas has many liars come forward. His problem is that the liars are not good enough to make sure their testimonies matched.

It is no wonder Jesus remains silent. There is no legal call for him to respond to the confused and contradictory statements made against him. Eventually, two testimonies are presented that do agree on one point: "This fellow said, 'I am able to destroy the temple of God, and to build it in three days" (Matthew 26:61). With two witnesses—albeit false witnesses—finally in sync with each other, this charge could be used as valid evidence against Jesus.

The High Priest Stood Up

That is why, at this crucial moment, the high priest suddenly "stood up." That small detail about Caiaphas' change in posture represents a key turning point in the trial. His *standing up* against Jesus recalls the Old Testament theme of the wicked standing up against the righteous, giving false testimony against him and asking him what he knows not, seeking to bring him to his death (see Psalm 27:12, 35:11, 86:14; Wisdom 2:12-20).[30] The high priest, therefore, is revealed to be in the role of the wicked who stand up against the innocent.

Mark also tells us that the high priest stood up "in the midst" of the council, showing his authority and the important role he is about to play in the hearing. He is signaling that he is taking control of the unraveling situation and "positioning himself to speak for the whole Sanhedrin to Jesus."[31] Caiaphas wants to seize the moment and take advantage of this slightest of openings in the proceedings and press Jesus for a response. He hopes Jesus will say something that they can use against him:

---

[30] Brown, *Death of the Messiah,* 1:434, 462.
[31] Ibid., 1:462.

"Have you no answer to make? What is it that those men testify against you?" (Matthew 26:62).

Yet Jesus does not play Caiaphas' game. He remains silent. In fact, the actual language Mark's Gospel uses to report Jesus' silent response is strong. It could be translated Jesus "stayed silent" and "answered nothing at all." The language emphasizes Christ's refusal to cooperate with the high priest. The trial is bogus. The council has sought false testimonies. All but two of those false testimonies have not panned out well. Even the accusation about Jesus' words regarding the Temple is itself not completely accurate. At least from the only New Testament record we have of Jesus making a statement similar to this accusation, Jesus does not say that he himself would destroy the Temple. He is certainly not claiming to be a terrorist out to obliterate the house of the Lord. He only prophesied that the Temple *would* be destroyed (see John 2:21).[32]

It is not surprising, therefore, that Jesus "stayed silent" and "answered nothing at all." The whole trial is a farce. As Raymond Brown observed: "The emphatic silence of ... Jesus is a contemptuous rebuke for the low quality of the charade."[33] Jesus' silence also fulfills the prophecy about the suffering servant of the Lord who remained quiet before his accusers: "Like a lamb led to the slaughter, he opened not his mouth" (Isaiah 53:7; Psalm 38:13-15).

Put Under Oath

The high priest makes a second attempt to get Jesus to say something self-incriminating. "Again the high priest asked him, 'Are you the Christ? The Son of the Blessed?'" (Mark 14:61). This

---

[32] The only thing he talked about happening in three days was the resurrection of his body: "'Destroy this temple and in three days I will raise it up'... But he spoke of the temple of his body" (John 1:19, 21). In other words, Jesus' statement about the Temple being destroyed and rebuilt in three days was primarily a symbolic foreshadowing of his death and resurrection. Ironically, while Jesus was speaking about his dying and rising, the false witnesses accuse him of speaking about the temple building.

[33] Brown, *Death of the Messiah,* 1:463.

time, the high priest uses the strongest possible authoritative language, putting Jesus under oath. "I adjure you, by the living God, tell us if you are the Christ, the Son of God" (Matthew 26:63).

This is what prompts Jesus to break his silence. The word adjure (*exorkizein*) is courtroom language describing someone being put under oath in order to secure testimony. It is similar to the King of Israel who put the prophet Micaiah under oath to compel him to give an answer that is true, saying: "How many times shall *I adjure you* that you speak to me nothing but the truth *in the name of the LORD*?" (1 Kings 22:14-16, emphasis added).[34]

Moreover, the high priest's expression "by the living God" echoes God's own oath formula: "As I live, says the Lord..."[35] The expression is also used as an oath by humans. The prophet Micaiah, for example, once used it in an attempt to emphasize the truthfulness of his words: "As the LORD lives, what the LORD says to me, that I will speak"(1 Kings 22:14; see also 1 Samuel 14:39). Moreover, according to Jewish tradition, if someone is put under oath by the divine name or a divine quality, he is bound.[36] The high priest, therefore, uses the strongest possible language to get Jesus to speak. His words, in fact, could be translated, "I put you under solemn oath before the living God to tell us if you are the Christ, the Son of God."[37] Imposing an oath before God, the high priest demands Jesus to answer.

"You Have Said So"

Under the forced oath, Jesus finally speaks: "You have said so" (Matthew 26:64).

[34] R.T. France, *The Gospel of Matthew* (Grand Rapids, MI: Eerdmans, 2007), 1024. He notes how demons are put under this authority during exorcisms (Mark 5:7; Acts 19:13), and how according to Josephus, the patriarch Joseph put his brothers under oath to bring his bones back to the land of Canaan.

[35] Ibid; see also Donald Senior, *The Passion Narrative According to Matthew* (Leuven, Netherlands: Leuven University Press, 1975), 174-175.

[36] Mishna *Sebu'ot* 4:13. Brown, *Death of the Messiah*, 1:465.

[37] John Nolland, *The Gospel of Matthew* (Grand Rapids, MI: Eerdmans, 2005), 1116.

Have you ever wondered what this expression means? In saying, "You have said so," Jesus neither agrees nor disagrees. The expression is what scholars refer to as a *qualified* affirmative. There is some truth in the high priest's statement, but he must take responsibility for the way he interprets it and what he does with it.[38] When the high priest asks if Jesus is "the Messiah" and "Son of God," it is as if Jesus responds, saying: "Yes, but I don't mean what you mean by those words."

In the popular mindset of the day, the word Messiah, translated as *Christ* in Greek, carried nationalistic overtones. It could put Jesus in the categories of political ambition and a threat to Rome, which is far from what Jesus actually said about his messianic mission (see Matthew 16:16, 20-23). Jesus did not come to revolt against Roman occupation. By his death and resurrection, he came to free humanity from sin and death (see John 3:16-17). Caiaphas, however, is not interested in sincerely understanding Jesus. He is simply looking for a charge to bring against him. If he can get Jesus to make a messianic claim under oath, he has the ammunition to condemn him.

"But I Say to You ..."

Jesus is the Messiah, but not in the way Caiaphas is thinking. That is why Jesus next pushes back strongly. He says to the high priest: "*But I say to you ...*" Here, Jesus is about to draw the line. He is emphatically telling the high priest that there is a crucial difference between what he thinks about the messiah ("you have said so") and Jesus' own understanding of his messianic identity and mission ("But I tell you ...").

What Jesus says next stands as the watershed moment in the trial. It is going to lead the high priest to tear his garments and

---

[38] Jesus gives the same response when replying to Pilate's "Are you the King of the Jews?" (Matthew 27:11).

the whole Sanhedrin to accuse Jesus of blasphemy, condemn him to death, spit at him, and strike him. What did Jesus say that got him in so much trouble?

——————— **REFLECTION QUESTIONS** ———————

- *Jesus remains silent for most of the trial before the Sanhedrin. We can learn from his example in many ways. First, describe a time when you had an argument with a friend or family member that was hopelessly going nowhere or perhaps only getting worse. How might Jesus' example of silence have been a better way to go in that discussion?*

- *Second, St. Mother Teresa said, "God speaks in the silence of the heart." But we live in a culture of incessant noise and distraction. In what ways might God be calling you to build in more silence in your life, so you can hear his voice?*

- *Third, how much do you feel the need to speak all the time— at work, with friends, with family? What can you do to take more time to listen to others? To give space for others to contribute to a conversation or to truly understand where others are coming from before speaking?*

Chapter Seven

THE SON OF MAN FINALLY SPEAKS

The Vision of Daniel by Rembrandt van Rijn

Here is the provocative statement Jesus makes to the high priest—the one that will lead the Sanhedrin to condemn him to death: "Hereafter you will see the Son of man seated at the right hand of Power, and coming on the clouds of heaven" (Matthew 26:64).

At first glance, we might wonder, what is so horrible about these words? Why do they get Jesus into so much trouble? If we can understand Christ's statement from the first century Jewish background, we would realize that Jesus is quoting from the famous "son of man" prophecy of Daniel 7.

Here, I want to step back and unpack this complex prophecy for you. I am going to break it down, so you can understand it easily and appreciate what Jesus meant by quoting it to the high

priest and why the members of the Sanhedrin would have been
so upset by him doing so.

The Son of Man

In this passage, the prophet Daniel has a vision at night—
perhaps it could be described as a nightmare—in which he
sees four dreadful beasts devouring the land: a lion with wings,
a man-eating bear, a four-headed leopard, and a most-fierce
beast with ten horns and iron teeth. Suddenly, a mysterious
fifth figure appears in the dream—not a beast, but "one like a
son of man." At his arrival, the fourth beast is destroyed, and
the other beasts fade away, while the "son of man" emerges
triumphant and is given an everlasting dominion ruling over
all nations:

> I saw in the night visions,
> and behold, with the clouds of heaven
> there came one like a son of man
> and he came to the Ancient of Days
> and was presented before him.
> And to him was given dominion
> and glory and kingdom,
> that all peoples, nations, and languages
> should serve him;
> his dominion is an everlasting dominion,
> which shall not pass away,
> and his kingdom one,
> that shall not be destroyed. (Daniel 7:13-14)

What is the meaning of this mysterious vision? On one level,
this is an ominous prophecy foretelling centuries of suffering
and oppression for God's people. Daniel is told that the four
beasts represent four gentile kings who will rule over the Jews
(see Daniel 7:17). They are traditionally associated with the
four major empires that dominated the land for most of the six

centuries leading up to Christ: the Babylonian, Mede-Persian, Greek, and Roman Empires.

At the same time, the vision offers hope. There will be light at the end of the tunnel. The son of man is associated with the faithful people of God, the saints of the Most High, who will be persecuted by the four beasts but, in the end, will be rescued and receive the everlasting kingdom and dominion over all the earth (see Daniel 7:17, 27). The prophecy about the son of man, therefore, gave the people hope that one day they would emerge triumphant, liberated from their enemies, and given an everlasting kingdom over all the earth.

In summary, the vision in Daniel 7 is about the movement of God's people from suffering to hope; persecution to vindication; death to new life. Jesus referring to this prophecy in itself certainly would not be a problem. The passage stands out in the Old Testament for capturing the Jewish expectations that God would rescue them in their centuries-old plight under the gentiles.

What gets Jesus into trouble, however, is his referring to *himself* as the "Son of man"—and not just in general sense, but specifically as being "seated at the right hand of Power and coming on the clouds of heaven" (Matthew 26:64).

Who is this mysterious son of man? Following the four beasts who represent four kings ruling over their four kingdoms, the son of man stands as a fifth king over a fifth kingdom that triumphs over all the others: the kingdom of God. The son of man will have dominion over all nations and his reign shall never end (see Daniel 7:11-14; 17). With this kind of royal splendor, it is no wonder that a number of ancient Jews understood this son of man to be the prophesied king—the messiah.[39] By referring to himself as the son of man in Daniel 7, Jesus is telling the High Priest that he is, indeed, the long-awaited messiah-king.

---

[39] 1 Enoch 48:10; 52:4; Babylonian Talmud, Sanhedrin 98a; Numbers Rabbah 13:14.

Coming on the Clouds of Heaven

That is not all, for the son of man in Daniel 7 is not just an earthly messiah. He also can be seen as a heavenly, divine being "seated at the right hand of Power" and "coming on the clouds of heaven." In Scripture, clouds are often associated with a theophany, a manifestation of God's holy presence. Throughout Scripture, God sometimes draws near his people and makes his presence known visibly in the form of a cloud: descending on Mount Sinai when giving the Law, guiding the Israelites in a pillar of cloud through the desert, overshadowing the tabernacle where the people will worship, filling the Temple in Jerusalem, coming over the mountain where Jesus was transfigured, and carrying Jesus up to heaven at his ascension.

> They charge him with blasphemy—not something they would do for claiming to be a king.

When we read in Daniel 7 of the son of man "coming on the clouds of heaven," we should realize how significant of a statement that is. In the Old Testament, that is something only God can do.[40] Such a depiction, therefore, points to how the son of man is no ordinary man. This mysterious fifth king comes *like* a son of man, meaning he only appears to be a merely human figure—a son of Adam—but in reality, he is something more. He comes also as a divine being.

Now think about what this would mean for Jesus to call himself the son of man. He is not only affirming that he is the messiah; he is also implicitly pointing to his divinity as the heavenly "son of man seated at the throne of Power and coming on the clouds of heaven." That's clearly how the chief priests, scribes. and elders understood him. Dismayed, they all cry out, "Are you the Son of God then?" (Luke 22:70). They charge him with blasphemy—not something they would do

---

[40] Brant Pitre, *The Case for Jesus* (New York: Image, 2016), 143.

for merely claiming to be a king. A chief priest might vehemently disagree with Jesus claiming to be Israel's messiah, but no one would view such a claim as blasphemy—a direct insult against God, punishable by death. As Brant Pitre explains, "If Jesus is claiming to be a *divine* Messiah who will be seated on a heavenly throne (like God) and come in on the clouds of heaven (also like God), then the charge of blasphemy makes sense."[41]

Chief Beasts

Are you getting a sense of just how loaded Jesus' self-identification as the son of man really is? And yet, there is still one more level of meaning we must consider—one that turns the tables on the Sanhedrin and shows how Jesus is accusing his accusers. He is putting the chief priests on trial, while he will be the one who ultimately acts as the final judge.

We have seen how the whole vision of Daniel 7 is all about the movement from persecution to vindication, from oppression to exaltation. Indeed, the son of man is closely associated with God's faithful people who are persecuted by the four gentile kingdoms, but whom God will rescue and vindicate.

Think about what it would mean for Jesus to claim to be the son of man during his trial in which he is being persecuted by the Sanhedrin. Such a claim would be highly provocative, indeed. For if Jesus is the son of man representing the people persecuted by the four beasts, what is Jesus saying about the chief priests, scribes, and elders who are persecuting *him*? He is putting the Jerusalem leaders in the shameful role of the beasts in Daniel 7—the ones who persecute the son of man!

Can you feel the weight of what Jesus is doing? He is saying that the leaders of Jerusalem have become like the gentile monsters in Daniel's vision who have oppressed the Jews for centuries.

---

[41] Ibid., 161.

The chief priests have become the chief beasts.[42] Jesus simply could not have struck a lower blow to his accusers. Though he is on trial before the Sanhedrin and his own life is on the line, Jesus turns the tables and accuses his accusers, telling them he will be the one coming in judgment over them in the day when they will see "the Son of man coming on the clouds of heaven" (Matthew 26:64). It is no wonder they tear their robes, mock him, spit at him, slap him, and condemn him to death.

Blasphemy!

The sin of blasphemy is an action, thought, or speech that expresses contempt for God. In Scripture, the word blasphemy (*blasphēmein*) in general means to abuse or insult, but of the twenty-two times the term appears in the early Greek translation of the Old Testament (known as the Septuagint), it is used in reference to insulting the God of Israel.

There were times in his public ministry when Jesus was accused of blasphemy for doing or saying something that put himself on par with God. When he forgave a man in Capernaum of his sins, the scribes complained in their hearts, "It is blasphemy! Who can forgive sins but God alone?" (Mark 2:7). Similarly, when in Jerusalem, Jesus once said, "I and the Father are one" (John 10:30). The Jewish leaders there accused him of blasphemy and picked up stones to stone him to death—which was the punishment for such a crime. They explain their actions, saying: "We stone you for no good work but for blasphemy; because you, being a man, make yourself God" (John 10:30-33). They tried to arrest him that day, but he escaped from their midst (see John 10:39).

When Jesus on this night makes the divine claim to be the son of man "coming on the clouds of heaven" and seated at the right

---

[42] Christopher Wright, *Knowing Jesus Through the Old Testament* (Downers Grove, IL: InterVarsity, 1992), 152-153.

hand of God, the members of the Sanhedrin do not just hear Jesus speak what they believe to be blasphemy again in a public setting where he can easily elude them. This time, they have Jesus say these words under arrest, on trial before the Sanhedrin, and speaking under oath to the High Priest. This time, they can act and make moves to carry out the appropriate punishment for blasphemy, which is death (see Leviticus 24:11-16).

Tearing Robes

In horror over what Jesus just said, the high priest tore his robes. Such an action was a symbolic act expressing anger or mourning in general (see Genesis 37:29, 34; Joshua 7:6). It was also a response to something terrible one had heard spoken about the God of Israel (see Numbers 14:6; 2 Kings 18:37; Acts 14:14). The ritual act signified a distancing of oneself from the evil things heard. Later Jewish tradition taught that when blasphemy is spoken, "the judges stand up and tear their robes, and they may not mend them again."[43] For Caiaphas, it is a public gesture of horror over what he thinks is blasphemy.

The irony, however, is that Jesus has just spoken the truth. He is, indeed, the Messiah, the Son of God, and the son of man who will come on the clouds of heaven. Yet Caiaphas calls the truthful revelation of the Son of God blasphemy. As New Testament scholars Davies and Allison point out, "By declaring that the Son of God, who has spoken the truth, has blasphemed, is not the high priest himself ironically guilty of blasphemy?"[44] The fact that Caiaphas as the high priest tears his garments only adds to the irony, for according to the Law, this high priest is forbidden to tear his sacred vestments (see Leviticus 21:10). Caiaphas gives the appearance of protecting the Law, but we see him on this night several times showing disregard for God's Law himself.

---

[43] See France, *The Gospel of Matthew,* 1029.

[44] W.D. Davies and Dale C. Allison, *Matthew 19-28* (London: T&T Clark, 2004), 532.

Mocking Jesus

The Gospels report how Jesus suffers at this moment both physical and personal abuse from the chief priests, scribes, and elders. They spit on him, strike him, slap him, beat him, and cover his face, blindfolding him and saying, "Prophecy to us, you Christ. Who is it that struck you?" (Mathew 26:67-68; see also Mark 14:65; Luke 22:63-65). Spitting on someone was an act of contempt (see Job 30:9-10), and the punishment for those considered guilty (see Numbers 12:14; Deuteronomy 25:9). Jesus being slapped and spit at fulfills what was prophesied about the suffering servant who would save Israel: "I gave my cheeks to slaps ... I hid not my face from shame and spitting" (Isaiah 50:6).

This brings to its climax one central theme throughout this scene: the irony of this mock trial. How ironic it is that the Sanhedrin pass judgment on the One who will judge them and all of humanity on the last day. They accuse Jesus of breaking the law when they are the ones who disobey the Law of Moses by seeking false witnesses and by their high priest tearing his garments. They accuse Jesus of blasphemy for speaking the truth about his divine identity and in the process blaspheme the holy Son of God. They blindfold Jesus so that he cannot see and mock him for being a false prophet, yet they are the ones who cannot see. They fail to see how in their own mocking of Christ, they unwittingly play a part in his fulfilling the prophecy of Isaiah 50:6-7 about the suffering servant's cheeks being slapped, and his face being shamed and spit at.

On the other hand, the Passion narratives make clear that Jesus is a most truthful prophet. Step-by-step, Jesus's prophecies on this night all come true. He prophesied Judas' betrayal (see John 13:21-26). He foretold how the disciples would fall away and scatter (see Matthew 26:31). We will also see next, that Jesus predicted with great accuracy how Peter would deny him three times before the cock crows (see Luke 22:34).

Nails to the Heart

A religious sister once told me how she was more sorrowful about the mocking of Jesus than about his crucifixion. During Lent, she was asked by her community to teach on Christ's passion for the poor they were serving. When she came to this part about the chief priests spitting at Jesus and blindfolding him, saying, "Prophecy to us, you Christ. Who is it that struck you?" (Mathew 26:67-68), she began to weep. And on Palm Sunday, when asked to teach a second time on this passage, she cried again. She asked me, "Why do I keep crying at this part? I have heard the stories of Christ's passion each year since my childhood, but now, when I come to this scene, I feel so sad wondering, *Why do they have make fun of him like this? I'm so saddened by this, even more than when Jesus was nailed to the Cross.*"

What a beautiful insight from this sister. Indeed, it is one thing to do someone physical harm, to harm the body. It is another thing to attack their personhood, their character and who they are. The physical abuse of beating, scourging, and crucifying a man is horrendous enough, but the personal abuse of jeering a person and inviting others to join in the mocking is worse. It strikes at the core of a person, of who they are, not just a part of their body. It is an attack on their very personhood. While many Christians focus on the physical sufferings Jesus endured on Good Friday, this sister reminds us of the deeper affliction Jesus took on for our sins. He wasn't just nailed to a cross in his hands and feet. The harsh, ridiculing words of the Jewish leaders—the leaders of the people he came to save—drove nails into his heart as well.

——————— REFLECTION QUESTIONS ———————

- *Jesus suffers a torturous death on the Cross. But he also endures another kind of abuse: the chief priests slap Jesus, spit at him, and mock him. Which kind of abuse do you think caused Jesus more suffering? Why?*

- *St. Mother Teresa taught that when we talk about another person, we should be very careful with our words. It's as if we are holding that person in our hands. How careful are you when you talk about others? Do you sometimes fall into gossip, complaining about others, pointing out their faults, making fun of them?*

- *During the trial, various accusers give testimony telling half-truths about Jesus. But half-truths are not honest speech. How careful are you to always tell the truth and not speak deceitfully to others, whether at work, at home, or with friends? Have you ever allowed "half-truths" to creep into your speech? Why do we do this sometimes?*

Chapter Eight

PETER DENIES JESUS

Peter denies Jesus, engraving

Jesus was not the only one being accused that night. During Christ's hearing before the Sanhedrin, Peter found himself facing his own trial of sorts just outside the high priest's residence.

While the other disciples scattered, Peter wants to be close to Jesus on this night to see what will happen to his Lord. He was able to access Caiaphas' courtyard because he was with John, the beloved disciple, who was known to the high priest (see John 18:15-16). Peter is described as having "followed him at a distance" (Luke 22:54), a point which, as one commentator explains, is "an ominous anticipation of the coming failure of Peter's 'following of Jesus.'"[45] Following Jesus is a fundamental

---

[45] John Nolland, *Luke 18:35-24:53* (Grand Rapids, MI: Eerdmans, 2005), 1094.

characteristic of being a disciple,[46] and Peter himself had "left everything and followed him" when he was first called by Jesus (Luke 5:11). But now, Peter timidly follows Christ "from a distance," an indication of his caution and fear and that his commitment to the Lord is already starting to waiver.

The whole scene involves movement. There is the three-fold *physical* movement as Peter goes from the courtyard to the gate to the outside at each of his denials (see Matthew 26:69, 71, 75). There is also the movement in escalating accusations made against Peter. He is initially suspected of simply having been associated with Jesus, but as the night goes on, people start to accuse him of being one of Christ's disciples. "Certainly, you are one of them!" (Mark 14:70). And then, there is the three-fold movement of escalating denials—Peter's rejections of Jesus increasing in their seriousness and force.

First, a servant girl says to him, "You also were with Jesus the Galilean" (Matthew 26:69).[47] Peter responds evasively. He does not directly deny the person of Jesus, but he denies understanding the woman's statements. "I do not know what you mean" (Matthew 26:70). Still, this is a decisive turning away from his discipleship, for being *with* Jesus is a key aspect of Christ's establishing the twelve apostles: "And he appointed twelve to be *with him*, and to be sent out to preach" (Mark 3:14, emphasis added). Peter himself, just earlier this same night, promised Jesus, "Lord, I am ready to go with you to prison and to death" (Luke 22:33). Now he denies he had ever been with Christ as one of the disciples.

"I Do Not Know the Man" (Matthew 26:72)

Peter then moves to the gateway of the courtyard, hoping to avoid further interrogation from the woman. Perhaps he also

---

[46] See Luke 5:27-28; 9:23; 10:57, 59, 61.

[47] Mark and Luke also mention a servant girl accusing Peter of being associated "with" Jesus (see Mark 14:67; Luke 22:56).

wants to get himself in a position to flee easily if things get worse. But he cannot escape another servant girl recognizing him. A second similar accusation is made about Peter's association with Jesus, but this time, Peter's denial is more direct and more forceful. It is more direct in the sense that he does not just claim lack of understanding over what is being said about him. When responding to this new accusation—"This man was with Jesus of Nazareth"—Peter flat out denies it: "I do not know the man" (Matthew 26:72).

For first century Jewish ears, Peter's words of denial are severe ones. They recall statements made against people who were expelled from the synagogue: "We no longer know you."[48] And Peter's words of denial take on even greater force because he speaks them under oath. Unlike Jesus who was put under oath by the high priest, Peter voluntarily puts himself under oath to make his denial. No one asked him to do so. There was no need to do so. The irony here is that Jesus taught his disciples never to take oaths: "Do not swear at all…" (Matthew 5:34-37). Yet Peter, who is supposed to be the leading disciple, completely disregards Jesus' teaching on this topic and swears an oath to deny his Lord.

After some time passes, a third accusation is made against Peter. Someone notices his Galilean dialect. "Certainly, you also are one of them, for your accent betrays you" (Matthew 26:73; see also Mark 14:70). The mounting pressure of these accusations is too much for Peter. This last one triggers in him the gravest denial of them all. Peter puts himself under a maledictory curse as he swears, "I do not know the man" (Matthew 26:74; see also Mark 14:71). Think about how much has changed in Peter since he arrived at the high priest's courtyard this night. He came in following Jesus "from a distance." Now, that distance just got a lot farther as he not only leaves the residence where Jesus is being detained but also rejects him under oath and puts himself under a curse.

---

[48] Davies and Allison, 547. See also Bock's comments on the parallel passage in Luke 22:57. Darrell L. Bock, *Luke 9:51-24:53* (Grand Rapids, MI: Baker, 2008), 1783.

The Lord looked at Peter, Church of Saint Peter in Gallicantu, Jerusalem

STEP ONE: Facing Our Sin

"The Lord Looked at Peter"

In the Church of St. Peter in Gallicantu in Jerusalem—the church traditionally believed to be built over Caiaphas' house—we find three beautiful icons that depict scenes related to Peter's denials. I like guiding pilgrims through these images because these three moments in Peter's journey as a disciple point to three crucial steps we need to take in our own.

The first icon portrays the moment of Peter's final denial, when Jesus "turned and looked at Peter" (Luke 22:61). Peter suddenly realizes what he has been doing. He remembers Jesus' prediction that he would deny Christ three times before the cock crows.

Have you ever wondered what kind of look Jesus gave Peter at that moment? Was it a look of anger, scorn, and wrath? Or was it a look of disappointment or displeasure that his leading disciple let him down? Or was it simply a look that said, "I told you so"? How would you feel if you were Peter, and Jesus looked at you at this moment?

The icon itself depicts Jesus gazing at Peter with a very serious look—which is fitting for this scene. Peter has just committed a very serious deed, one that cannot be overlooked or brushed aside. It must be addressed. Jesus looks at Peter to call him on it—not in a "pointing fingers" kind of way, or out of condemnation, but for Peter's own good. The look immediately wakes Peter out of his fear of being exposed in the high priest's courtyard and he suddenly realizes the truth of what he has been doing. This points to a crucial first step in the spiritual life that we must take over and over again: to face the honest truth of our actions—the ways we hurt others, the ways we hurt our relationship with God, and the truth of our sins and weaknesses.

In the icon, some pilgrims also notice a touch of *sadness* in Jesus' eyes. This, too, makes sense, for I am sure Jesus felt sad for Peter—for Peter's weakness, for Peter's turning away from him, for how distraught Peter must be feeling. In the end, I think Jesus looked at Peter with great love, like he did with the rich young man who walked away from discipleship. That man sincerely wanted to follow Jesus but was too attached to his possessions and refused. Nevertheless, Jesus "looking upon him loved him" (Mark 10:21).

Jesus' look of love for Peter and the rich young man is comforting for us. It reminds us that no matter how deeply or how often we fall, we remain beloved in God's eyes. He looks at us not with a condemning look, but a look of love. That gives us the space and confidence to face the truth about ourselves, so that we can repent with contrite hearts, which is the next step exhibited by Peter that night.

Peter went out and wept, Church of Saint Peter in Gallicantu, Jerusalem

STEP TWO: Sorrow for Sin

"He Wept Bitterly" (Luke 22:62)

The second icon portrays Peter's deep sorrow: "And he went out and wept bitterly" (Luke 22:62). In the icon, Peter is siting all alone, curled up a bit. Isolated. Looking down. Looking forlorn. His hand holds up his drooping head.

The word Luke uses to describe Peter having "wept" (*klainein*) expresses a very emotional response. About half of the twenty-one uses of this word describe someone wailing over the deceased (see Luke 8:52; John 11:31, 33). That may be significant for understanding Peter's response here. Peter is grieving tremendously—as if someone has just died. Indeed, something inside Peter has died: his discipleship, his faithfulness, his friendship with Jesus, and his promise to go with him even to prison and to death. Peter mourns over his denials of Jesus so intensely, it is like one mourning over the loss of a loved one.

At this heart-rending moment, Peter comes face-to-face with the truth about himself and his tragic actions this night. There is no room for softening his denials, blaming others, making excuses or pretending it is not that big of a deal. He realizes the magnitude of his sin and the damage he has caused in his relationship with the one he loves. As a result, he "wept bitterly." And this all points to a second important step in the spiritual life: *sorrow for our sins.*

This sorrow entails much more than an apology. A truly contrite heart acknowledges one's sin and is sorrowful over the sin itself. The sorrow is not focused on oneself—being upset over one's weakness or being afraid of what others might think or over the consequences one might face.

> **Peter comes face-to-face with the truth about himself and his tragic actions this night.**

Rather, a repentant heart detests the sin itself as an offense against the Lord and remains focused on the ways one has hurt his relationship with God and others. In Peter's case, all his attention is on his having denied his Lord. As he was weeping bitterly over his sin, Peter might have recalled the famous psalm of repentance in the Jewish Scriptures—Psalm 51—which is a prayer that would have quite fittingly expressed the kind of contrite heart Peter had that night.

> Have mercy on me, O God,
> according to thy steadfast love;
> According to thy abundant mercy
> Blot out my transgressions.
> Wash me thoroughly from my iniquity,
> and cleanse me from my sin!
> For I know my transgressions,
> and my sin is ever before me.
> Against thee only, have I sinned,
> and done what is evil in thy sight. (Psalm 51:1-4)

"Peter, do you love me?" Church of Saint Peter in Gallicantu, Jerusalem

STEP THREE: Encountering Mercy

"Do You Love Me?" (John 21:15-19)

The third icon depicts a scene after the Resurrection, when Jesus approaches Peter along the shores of the Sea of Galilee. The artist imagines Jesus making direct eye contact with Peter again—perhaps for the first time since he turned and looked at him on Holy Thursday night. Imagine that moment for Peter!

This scene represents a third important step in the spiritual life: *encountering God's mercy*. And it challenges us to ask a question: When we sin, do we look at ourselves, or do we look upon the Lord? Too often, we remain stuck in the phase depicted by the second icon. We are looking down at our sin, frustrated with ourselves. Sorrowful? Yes, but are we more sorrowful over having offended God? Or are we upset over our not being as good or as holy as we think we should be? There is a big difference between these two kinds of sorrow.

Sometimes when we realize our failures and weaknesses, especially when we find ourselves repeatedly struggling with the same sins, we can become upset and discouraged. We are easily frustrated and say, "I can't believe I did that! Why am I not better?"

On the surface, such a response might appear as humility, but in reality, we may be exhibiting a form of spiritual pride. We are not so focused on our relationship with God but are too focused on ourselves. What troubles us is not so much that we have offended the Lord, but that the ideal image we would like to have of ourselves has been smashed. Notice the focus on self. "I can't believe *I* did that!" That is why we need to move from the second icon to the third—from looking down at our sins and weaknesses to looking up at the loving gaze of Jesus. Peter "wept bitterly" over his sins, but he did not stay weeping and looking down at himself forever. He eventually looked up and encountered Jesus gazing at him with gentleness, mercy, and love. From that encounter, Peter became a changed man. He was transformed and became the strong rock Christ intended him to be for the Church. None of that would have happened if Peter remained stuck at the second icon, looking down at his sin.

In this scene depicted by the third icon, Jesus asks Peter three times, "Do you love me?" He gives Peter the chance to reaffirm his love for Christ and to undo his three-fold denials on Holy Thursday night. There is something deeper happening in this scene that ties all three icons together and sheds much light on the kind of encounter Jesus wants to have with us in our weakness and the transformation he wants to work in our lives—if we dare to look up.

Do You Love Me?

Let's take a close look at the very personal question Jesus asks Peter: "Do you love me?" At first glance, we might think this is just a basic question, and one to which we would expect Peter to give a whole-hearted, "Yes!" But the word used for love here in John's Gospel would make Peter pause. The word is related to the Greek term *agape*, which is a lot more than ordinary human affection. Another Greek word, *philea*, describes that kind of love. *Agape*, however, describes perfect, total, self-giving love—the kind of love Jesus models on the Cross.

Earlier in his career, sanguine, overconfident Peter probably would have said he loved Jesus with *agape* love. Recall Peter's bravado at the Last Supper when he said he would go anywhere with Christ, even to prison and to death.

But this is a different Peter. An honest Peter. A humbled, devastated Peter, who has painfully grown in self-knowledge. After his three-fold denials on Holy Thursday night, there is no way Peter can pretend to live *agape* love. He affirms a kind of love for Jesus, but uses the word related to *philea*, not *agape*, to describe it. It is as if he says to Jesus, "You of all people know how incapable I am of that higher *agape* love. The best I can offer you, Jesus, is my weak, imperfect, messy human love: *philea*. Peter is learning to come to Jesus as he really is.

Jesus presses in and asks Peter the same question a second time, "Do you love me?" And Peter once again, humbled by the very question, gives the same honest response. When Jesus asks a third time, he changes the word for love. He does not lower the standard, but he comes down to meet Peter where he is at and asks if Peter loves him with *philea* love. It is as if he says: "Peter, I will take your weak, imperfect human love. I will take whatever love you offer me."

This beautiful moment represents a crucial turning point in Peter's life. Now that Peter is willing to come to Jesus as he really is, with all his weaknesses, Jesus will act in a profound way. He will take Peter's imperfect *philea* love and transform it into *agape*. From this point on, Peter will be a changed man. In fact, Jesus immediately gives a prophecy about Peter's future martyrdom. He tells Peter that one day "you will stretch out your hands ... and another will carry you where you do not wish to go" (John 21:18). This points to how Peter will eventually go to Rome, where his arms will be stretched out on a cross when he is crucified in Nero's circus. Peter will, indeed, live *agape* love. Though he denied Jesus to a few people outside Caiaphas' house,

> Jesus wants to meet the *real* you—not the you that you like to project.

he will boldly proclaim Christ to thousands and be willing to suffer, to be accused, to be imprisoned, and even to give the heroic witness of martyrdom for the sake of the gospel. Peter's key moment of conversion began right here on the shores of the Sea of Galilee when he finally came to Jesus without any pretense or inflated view of himself, but humbly in the truth of his glaring imperfections.

The same transformation God worked in Peter, he wants to do in all of us if we learn to be vulnerable with him, to allow him to love us as we are with all our inadequacies, dysfunction, wounds, and fears. After all, Jesus wants to meet the real you—not the you that you like to project to your family, coworkers, fellow parishioners, and social media friends, or the ideal one you hope to become someday; not even one you like to present to yourself to keep you from having to look under the hood and face what you might find inside. Only if we dare to come before the Lord regularly, as we really are, in our "Peter moments," can we encounter what Peter encountered that day: God's love, mercy, and healing grace that meets us in our imperfections and transforms us little-by-little into saints.

──────────── **REFLECTION QUESTIONS** ────────────

- *Imagine being Peter at the moment Jesus looks at him when the cock crowed. How would you feel at that moment? Now put yourself in Peter's shoes the next time Jesus talks to him—after the Resurrection, after Peter denied him three times. How would you feel when Jesus asks at that point, "Do you love me?" How would you respond?*

- *When we come to terms with our weaknesses and sins, we might be tempted to discouragement ("I'm such a mess!") or even despair ("It's too hard … I will never change"). How does Jesus' encounter with Peter after the Resurrection encourage you in the midst of your various struggles with living the Christian life?*

- *In this chapter, we saw how Jesus wants us to come to him as we really are—with all our weakness, wounds, and sins—like Peter finally did when they met again after Easter. Indeed, Jesus wants to meet the real you—not the one you wish you could be or the one you like to project to others. How comfortable are you coming before Jesus humble and vulnerable like this? What keeps you from doing this more fully and more often?*

Chapter Nine

JUDAS, THE BETRAYER

Judas betrays Jesus with a kiss

While Peter was weeping bitterly over his denials, Judas was lamenting his own sin of having betrayed Jesus. Matthew's Gospel tells us Judas deeply regretted what he had done (see Matthew 27:3).

Though sometimes translated as "repented," the actual Greek word Matthew uses to describe what was going on in Judas' heart is *metamelomai*. The word means having a change of feeling or a change with one's concern, which can be accompanied by sadness. It could be translated as "having changed with remorse." The idea is that Judas *deeply regretted* his actions.

This is a positive first step in Judas. He recognizes he has done something wrong, that he has sinned (see Matthew 27:4). As darkened as Judas had become, Pope Benedict XVI points out "the light shed by Jesus into Judas' soul was not completely extinguished ... Everything pure and great that he had received from Jesus remained inscribed on his soul—he could not forget it."[49]

Still, his remorse did not lead him to turn his life around and turn to God. He falls short of repentance. In fact, Matthew avoids the usual word for repentance (*metanoein*), which describes a decisive change in heart and mind, a fundamental change of direction in life. Judas is filled with remorse, but he does not actually repent (*metanoein*). He feels horribly about what he has done. He takes a step toward conversion, admitting that he had sinned and that he had betrayed "innocent blood" (Matthew 27:4). He even throws the money back at the chief priests—a tangible way of trying to dissociate himself with his treacherous deed. Judas clearly hates what he has done. But he does not turn to God when expressing his sorrow. He is focused only on himself and his sin.

Regret Versus Repent

There is a big difference between regret and repentance. A politician might regret a sin from his past that gets exposed. But he might regret it merely because it hurts his reputation. It is bad for public relations. That does not mean he has *repented* of his sin in the sense of making a decisive change in his life, turning away from sin and turning to God.

Similarly, take a marriage relationship. If, for example, I speak some impatient words to my wife, it is one thing for me merely to regret those words. *Oh no. I wish I didn't say that. I'm in trouble now. She's mad at me.* I might also regret my words because I am mad at myself for my mistakes. *Why do I keep doing dumb things like that? I'm so mad at myself. Why can't I be a better husband?* Notice how these responses of mere regret are not focused on my wife and our relationship. They are focused on me.

---

[49] Benedict XVI, *Jesus of Nazareth: Holy Week*, 68-69.

A truly repentant heart, however, is focused on the person we love, the person we have hurt and our relationship. *I love my wife and feel badly that I hurt her with these words. She deserves so much better than this. I am going to tell her how sorry I am and to try my best not to do anything like that again.*

In sum, regret on its own is often focused on either one's own self-interest (I regret what I did because of the consequences) or on self-condemnation (I regret what I did because it reminds me of how imperfect I am). True repentance, however, is focused on the other person and the relationship.

When we sin against God, we need to have much more than self-centered regret. We need to turn our eyes to the Lord and tell him, "I'm sorry Jesus. I love you. I don't want to hurt my relationship with you. I beg for your grace to help me not do this again."

The Difference Between Peter and Judas

Think about the differences between Peter and Judas. Both deny Christ on Holy Thursday night. Why does one story end in reconciliation and new life, while the other ends in despair and death? First, Peter's sin, though horrific, is not as grave as Judas' sin. Peter sins in his words, spontaneously, under tremendous pressure. He did not enter the high priest's court intending to deny his Lord. Judas' sin, however, was premeditated. He thought through his plan and intentionally sought out the chief priests to betray Jesus and gain thirty pieces of silver.

Despite the seriousness of Judas' sin, it would not have kept him from reconciliation with Jesus if he simply had turned to God— if he *repented* and trusted in God's mercy. Instead, Judas merely *regretted* what he did. He focused on himself and his horrific crime. "I have sinned in betraying innocent blood!" (Matthew 27:4). What Judas does with the realization of his sin is very different from what Peter did when he heard the cock crow. And Matthew's Gospel uses one small word to make a subtle point highlighting this difference: the word "went." Matthew notes how both Peter and Judas, at the moment they realized their sin, "went" out from the place where the chief priests were gathered. But they each "went" in very different directions. Peter *went* out (*exelthōn*) and *wept* bitterly. Judas, however, *went* (*apelthōn*) and *hanged* himself (see Matthew 26:75; 27:5).

Why Did Judas Betray Jesus?

How could the story of a disciple of Jesus end so tragically? What was it that drove Judas to betray his Lord?

The Bible suggests that, in part, it had to do with money. We know from John's Gospel that Judas was the treasurer for the group but had been a thief, taking money for himself and not caring for the poor (see John 12:6). This is why he was so upset over Mary of Bethany anointing the feet of Jesus with a lavish amount of costly ointment, asking, "Why was this ointment not sold for three hundred denarii?" (John 12:5). Judas seems to have been hoping for access to that money for himself. His greed, in the end, even drove him to ask the chief priests how much money they would give him if he delivered Jesus to them. Judas took their offer of thirty pieces of silver in exchange for betraying Christ (see Matthew 26:15).

There may also be some clues in his name, Judas "Iscariot," which may identify him as "a man of Kerioth"—probably referring to the village near Hebron mentioned twice in the Old Testament (see Joshua 15:25; Amos 2:2). This implies Judas was from the southern region of Judah, making him the only one of the twelve apostles not from Galilee. Others interpret Iscariot as "the assassin" (from the Greek word *sikarios*). This has led some to posit that Judas was sympathetic with the violent revolutionary movements and was upset that Jesus' ministry did not correspond to his political hopes for the kingdom.

Whatever human motivations there may have been, the Gospels make clear that Satan was at work. John notes that during the Last Supper, "the devil had already put into the heart of Judas Iscariot … to betray him" (John 13:2). Luke tells how "Satan entered into Judas" and he went to confer with the chief priests about how to betray Christ (Luke 22:3). At the most important moment in Jesus' life, Judas gave in to the temptations of the Evil One.

Such dramatic falls like this, however, do not happen out of the blue. As Archbishop Fulton Sheen once wrote, "There must also be an interior failure before there can be an outward one."[50]

> "There must also be an interior failure before there can be an outward one."
> —Archbishop Fulton J. Sheen

He and others have pointed out that something happened a year earlier when Passover was near that indicates Judas already was having difficulties in following Jesus.

"One of You Is a Devil"

After Jesus multiplied the loaves and fed the 5,000, the people wanted to carry him off and make him king (see John 6:15). Jesus had reached a peak in his popularity, and his movement was on a roll. But Jesus ran away from the crowds' more political view of kingship, and the next day, he gave a teaching that sent his public approval ratings plummeting. Many in those same enthusiastic crowds suddenly rejected Jesus, and even some of Jesus' own disciples left him over this issue.

What did Jesus say that was so upsetting? He taught about the Eucharist, saying people must eat his flesh and drink his blood

---

[50] Fulton Sheen, *The Life of Christ* (New York: McGraw-Hill, 1958), 301.

if they want to have eternal life (see John 6:51-56). The crowds were confused and angry. "How can this man give us his flesh to eat?" (John 6:52). Even many of Jesus' own disciples could not accept this teaching and turned away from him that day (see John 6:66). Jesus let them go.

Jesus even turned to his twelve apostles and asked if they would leave also. Peter gives an excellent response. He does not claim to have enlightened theological understanding about Jesus' Eucharistic teachings; he actually seems just as puzzled as everyone else that day. But his faith is not shaken. What makes Peter's response so exemplary is that he trusts Jesus more than he trusts himself. "Lord, to whom shall we go? You have the words of eternal life" (John 6:68). It is as if he is saying, "Lord, I have no idea what you are talking about, but I trust you."

Not all the twelve, however, had such faith that day. Right at this moment, Jesus makes a cryptic statement to them indicating there is one who does not believe. He speaks figuratively about one of them being a devil, "Did I not choose you, the twelve, and one of you is a devil?" (John 6:70). John's Gospel then informs the reader which apostle Jesus had in mind. "He spoke of Judas the son of Simon Iscariot, for he, one of the twelve, was to betray him" (John 6:71).

This is the first time in the Gospels that we read about Jesus expressing concerns about Judas. What just happened that made Jesus say this? We do not know for sure, but John's Gospel seems to hint that there were two things that rattled Judas that day: Christ's teachings on the Eucharist, and the crowds abandoning him over that teaching. On this day, one year before the Last Supper, Jesus cryptically speaks about Judas being a devil. Perhaps Judas did not like Jesus turning away from being a popular king. Maybe he became disenchanted over Jesus' teachings on the Eucharist and how it caused his movement to lose steam. He may have been tempted to leave Christ with the other fallen-away disciples. Perhaps Judas left Jesus in his heart that day but strove to maintain the outward appearance of a disciple. Whatever the case, we know that one year later, on the next Passover, Judas will leave definitively—when he leaves the table where Jesus institutes the Eucharist to go to the chief priests to betray him.

───── REFLECTION QUESTIONS ─────

- *When tires go flat, it's usually because of a small leak, not a big blow out. The same is true in the Christian life. Big sins usually don't come out of nowhere. They typically are the result of smaller sins—small acts of infidelity—that build up over time. What were some of the "small leaks" in Judas' life that led to his betrayal of Christ?*

- *Both Peter and Judas committed serious sins on Holy Thursday night. Why is one reconciled with God and given a fresh start in life while the other ends in death?*

- *What is the difference between merely regretting something and repenting of it? Describe a time when you regretted doing something but didn't repent.*

Chapter Ten

BEFORE PILATE: WHAT IS TRUTH?

Pilate washes his hands

Early in the morning, members of the Sanhedrin plot their next move. They had successfully charged Jesus with blasphemy in their sham proceedings the night before. According to the Jewish law, blasphemy is to be punished with death, but they still face one major obstacle. Under Roman rule, the Jews are not allowed to carry out capital punishment. Only the local Roman authorities could do that. They need to bring Jesus to the local governor of Judea—a man named Pontius Pilate—and convince him that Jesus deserves to die.

What charge will they bring against him? Pilate is not going to care about accusations of blasphemy or Jesus' statements about the Temple or his claims about being the son of man coming on the clouds of heaven. These are religious matters for the Jewish leaders to address, not a concern for the Roman governor of Judea. This is why the Sanhedrin needs to carefully strategize their next step with Pilate: "The chief priests and elders of the people took counsel against Jesus to put him to death" (Matthew 27:1).

Taking Counsel Against Christ

This description of them *taking counsel* against Jesus recalls a prophecy in the messianic Psalm 2 about how the rulers will "take counsel" together against the messiah, the Lord's anointed one. "Why do the nations conspire, and the peoples plot in vain? The kings of the earth set themselves and the rulers *take counsel* together, against the LORD and his anointed" (Psalm 2:1-2, emphasis added).

Just as Psalm 2 foretold, the leaders conspire against the Lord's anointed one as they "took counsel" on how to destroy him. Matthew's Gospel makes this connection three times during Jesus' last week in Jerusalem:

> The Pharisees "took counsel against Jesus," trying to "entangle him in his talk" (Matthew 22:15).

> The chief priests and elders gathered at Caiaphas' house and "took counsel" about how to arrest Jesus by stealth (Matthew 26:3-4).

> Now, they assemble one more time to take "counsel against Jesus" and plot their final move: convincing Pilate to have Jesus be executed (Matthew 27:1).

Before Pilate

When they bring Jesus to Pilate, everything is carefully choreographed. The chief priests have Jesus bound like a serious criminal, probably to give the appearance that he is more of a threat to Rome than he really is (see Matthew 27:2). And when they deliver him over to Pilate, they come in numbers.

The Gospels note how "all" the chief priests and elders, "the whole company of them" brought him to Pilate (Matthew 27:1; Luke 23:1). Their coming in solidarity as a large block adds to the impression that there is some serious danger, some urgent matter that the Roman Governor needs to address at once.

They proceed to "accuse" Jesus (Luke 23:2). The word for "accuse" here is a technical term used in court settings to present a formal legal charge against someone. The chief priests and scribes make three such accusations against Jesus, all of which are intended to make Jesus out to be someone who is undermining Roman rule.

First, they tell Pilate that Jesus is "perverting" or "leading astray" the nation in the sense of leading them away from their proper loyalty to Rome.[51] Second, they falsely accuse Jesus of discouraging people from paying taxes to Caesar—which is what they tried to trick Jesus into saying, but he had never said that (see Luke 20:20-26). Third, they charge Jesus with claiming to be a messiah king in the sense of someone aspiring to royal authority and toppling Roman rule.

Notice how these were not the accusations the chief priests made against Jesus the night before. There was no mention of the Temple, the Son of Man, the clouds of heaven, or the Son of God. They knew Pilate would not care about those matters, so they pivot their message to focus on new kinds of allegations that might grab his attention. Their plan worked. Though Pilate seems skeptical of their charges, he does latch on to one issue—that Jesus claims to be "messiah, a king." He begins his line of questioning of Jesus with, "Are you the King of the Jews?" (Luke 23:3).

---

51 From a Jewish biblical perspective, the description of Jesus as "leading astray" the people wrongly portrays him as a "false prophet," but for readers of the Gospels, it also brings to mind Moses and Elijah, who were wrongly accused by pagan rulers of "leading astray" the people of Israel (Exodus 5:4; 1 Kings 18:17).

"Are You the King of the Jews?" (Luke 23:3)

Jesus answers Pilate like he answered the high priest, "You have said so." We saw earlier how this expression is a *qualified* affirmative that basically means, "Yes, but I don't mean what you mean by those words." Jesus is a king, but not in the way Pilate or the chief priests think. He is not aspiring to political power or starting a revolt, which is what the people commonly hoped for in a messiah-king in first-century Judaism. Jesus' kingship is different. His movement is not the kind of threat to the Roman Empire that other ambitious Jewish messiahs might have been. In John's account of this scene, Jesus later goes on to make this point clear. Jesus is a true king, but his "kingship is not of this world" (John 18: 36).

When the chief priests accuse Jesus before the Roman governor, Jesus remains silent, refusing to answer any of the charges (see Matthew 27:14). Without offering a defense, Jesus still leaves quite an impression with Pilate. Matthew's Gospel tells us that Pilate was "surprised" or "wondered greatly" (Matthew 27:14). The word for surprised (*thaumazō*) is used in Matthew's Gospel to describe someone who is *positively* surprised

> Pilate is used to dealing with revolutionaries … and he knows Jesus is not one of them.

or impressed. It describes how Jesus marvels over the faith of the Roman Centurion (Matthew 8:10); how the crowds were amazed by Christ's miracles (see Matthew 8:27, 9:33, 15:31), and how the people were greatly impressed by his teaching (see Matthew 22:22). Pilate senses there is something different about Jesus and "wonders greatly" about him.

Pilate also quickly realizes Jesus is innocent. After all, Pilate is used to dealing with revolutionaries. He knows what a real revolutionary looks like, and he knows Jesus is not one of them. Jesus may have grass roots popularity as a Jewish teacher, but he is not a real threat to Rome. Pilate realizes that the real issue is a religious dispute between Jesus and the chief priests and that "it was out of envy that they had delivered him up" (Matthew 27:18). The last thing he wants to do is enter into that fray and allow the chief priests to exploit his authority for their own political advantage. That is why his initial response to their accusations is to declare Jesus innocent. "I find no crime in this man" (Luke 23:4).

The chief priests will not back down. They, in fact, ratchet up the accusations against Jesus. They say Jesus was "stirring up" the people throughout Galilee, Judea, and Jerusalem—painting a picture of him as spreading widespread unrest across the land (see Luke 23:5). The implication is that Jesus is inciting the people against Roman rule. Should not the Roman governor be concerned about that?

Herod Hears Nothing

At this, Pilate realizes securing Jesus' release will not be easy. The chief priests are not going to back down. They continue pressing Pilate with charges that Jesus is leading the people away from their loyalty to Rome. What can Pilate do?

One detail Pilate learns about Jesus, however, gives him an idea. When Pilate hears Jesus is from Galilee, he sees a way out of his dilemma because Galilee is in Herod's jurisdiction. He can pass the buck to Herod, who happens to be in town for the Passover festival. Since Jesus is a Galilean, Pilate will let Herod deal with this problem.

Herod was thrilled at this opportunity, "for he had long desired to see him, because he had heard about him, and he was hoping to see some sign done by him" (Luke 23:8, 9:7-9). At first glance, the reader might interpret this as good fortune for Jesus—he is being handed over to a fan, someone eager to see him, hear his teaching, and witness some miraculous sign. The language also recalls what Jesus said about his disciples:

that *kings* have longed to see and hear what they as disciples *see* and *hear* in his ministry (see Luke 10:24).

The careful reader of Luke's Gospel will hear an ominous note, however. For the description about Herod "hoping to see some sign" recalls how those who seek a sign from Jesus are part of the evil generation (see Luke 11:16, 29-30). Herod does not approach Jesus humbly, wanting to learn from him like true disciples who "hear the word of God and do it" (Luke 8:21). He instead treats Jesus like a performer and just wants to witness something spectacular. As a result, he fails to see and hear what Jesus has to offer the world.

Ironically, Herod, in fact, hears nothing at all from Jesus, for Jesus remains silent before him, refusing to say a single word. Jesus once again fulfills the prophecy about the suffering servant of the Lord before his accusers in that he "opened not his mouth" (Isaiah 53:7).

When We Are Like Herod

We might never mock Jesus like Herod ends up doing, but we might fall into the temptation of approaching Jesus primarily for what he can do for us—a wonder worker who can solve our problems and help us in our troubles. We sometimes treat Jesus like a spiritual Santa Claus. We do all the talking in prayer and present him all our wishes.

Do you take time to *listen* in prayer? Or do you tend to do all the talking? Do you seek to hear the voice of God in your life? A true disciple approaches Jesus humbly when presenting needs like the leper who said: "Lord if you will, you can make me clean" (Matthew 8:2), or Mary and Martha who when Lazarus was dying said, "Lord, he whom you love is ill" (John 11:3). Notice how they do not do all the talking. Neither do they tell Jesus what to do. They do not present a list of demands or problems with instructions on how to solve them. Rather, they humbly present their needs, and they also wait to listen to what Jesus will say and watch what he will do. They trust that Jesus will respond in the best way. A true disciple seeks to "hear the word of God and do it" (Luke 8:21, 11:28). A true disciple is like the Virgin Mary, someone who maintains interior space to hear the voice of God through the events unfolding in her life. She was someone who "kept all these things, pondering them in her heart" (Luke 2:19).

Luke ends the account by suddenly mentioning how another group of people are present with Herod. The throng of chief priests and scribes that handed Jesus over to Pilate have come to make sure Herod hears their accusations directly from them. They "stood by, vehemently accusing him" (Luke 23:10).

Having been rebuffed by Jesus, Herod lowers himself to the level of his soldiers who mock Jesus with contempt. He put a radiant robe on Jesus and sent him back to Pilate scornfully humiliated but not willing to accept responsibility for the fate of Jesus. Nevertheless, the scene ends with Luke commenting on how Herod and Pilate became friends that day—probably because Herod was flattered that Pilate involved him in the trial, and because both leaders came to the same conclusion about Jesus' innocence and the Jewish leaders' envy as the real motive for their accusations. This small level of cooperation and agreement on Good Friday seems to have broken down some longstanding tension between the two (see Luke 23:12).

A Wife's Dream

Pilate's own judgment led him to conclude that Jesus was innocent. Now he gets an extraordinary confirmation from his wife. She tells him that she had a dream that he should not do any harm to Jesus, whom she describes as "that righteous man" (Matthew 27:19). In the Old Testament and wider ancient world, dreams were often considered a means of divine guidance.

Ironically, this gentile woman sees things more accurately than the Jewish leaders in Jerusalem do. She testifies to Christ's innocence while the Sanhedrin declares him guilty.

What will her husband do? What will his final decision be? Pilate is like St. Joseph, the husband of Mary, who earlier in Matthew's Gospel received dreams from God. Both men receive a divine message through a dream. Both messages were about the protection of Jesus. The difference, however, is that Joseph obeyed the message and protected the Christ child. Pilate, however, will ignore the message. Instead of protecting the innocent Christ, he will give in to the pressure of the crowds and send Jesus off to be crucified.

What Is Truth?

As the events progress on Good Friday, Jesus at some point tells Pilate that he has come into the world to bear witness to the truth. It is then that Pilate responds with his remarkable sarcastic statement, "What is truth?" (John 18:38).

It is crucial that we understand the weight of what Pilate is saying here. For it is his understanding of truth—or perhaps it is more accurate to say, his *lack* of understanding of truth—that paves the way for the innocent Jesus to be crucified.

For Pilate, real truth—objective truth that is true for everyone—is not important. Pilate knows Jesus is innocent. He knows the facts. Jesus is not a real threat to Roman rule. He also knows this trial is really about the chief priest's envy and their desire to maintain power. But if there is no truth—if truth is relative—none of those facts matter. Pilate has "his own truth." He is left to his own self-interest on this difficult day. The chief priests start stirring up the crowds to call for Christ's crucifixion, and the people start threatening Pilate, saying, "If you release this man, you are not Caesar's friend; everyone who makes himself a king sets himself against Caesar" (John 19:12). It is too much for Pilate. He has no moral compass, *no truth*, to guide him in difficult decisions. He just does what is most expedient for his career. Pilot sends an innocent man off to be crucified in order to protect his own selfish interests.

That is what happens when a culture embraces Pilate's philosophy of "What Is Truth?" When a culture denies truth as a moral standard outside itself, many innocent people get hurt as we use it to justify the most horrific crimes.

Indeed, much of modern culture has embraced Pilate's philosophy of moral relativism—the idea that truth is relative. Every individual makes up his own truth, his own morality. Relativism says, "You can have *your* truth and I can have *my* truth, but there is no *the* truth to which we are all accountable." Like Pilate, many in our culture embrace moral relativism mistakenly thinking that it covers up a multitude of sins. If there is no right or wrong, I can continue doing whatever I want and not feel badly about it.

The problem is that if there is no truth, then anything goes. Anything can be rationalized and justified. Anything can be chosen as "good for me" no matter how much it hurts other people. Without truth, there is no compelling reason to put someone else's good before one's own self-interest.

For example, if we say there is no truth, then we cannot say that a father who leaves his wife and kids to run off with another woman is doing anything wrong. It can be construed as "good for him" as "his truth." If we say there is no truth, we cannot say that someone neglecting the poor and suffering while storing up riches for himself is doing anything wrong, because that is good for him and his truth. If we say there is no truth, then we cannot say that the killing of an untold number of babies, whether in child sacrifice in primitive cultures or in abortion in our own, is wrong—because each culture is free to make up its own truth and its own morality. With Pilate's philosophy of relativism, there is no truth, there is no good or evil, so we can never say anything is right or wrong.

We must remember, however, that truth is not an abstract concept. Truth is a Person—Jesus Christ. Jesus says he is "the Way, the Truth and the Life." To the extent we deny that there is an objective truth that applies to everyone, we not only hurt other people, we also do great harm to our own souls, for we are denying Christ himself.

REFLECTION QUESTIONS

- *Herod was very eager to meet Jesus, but he wasn't interested in learning from Jesus or living in friendship with him as a disciple. Herod only wanted to see Jesus perform a sign. How do you treat Jesus? Do you approach Jesus humbly, seeking his plan for your life? Or do you tend to come to him with a list of needs, telling him how to solve your problems and help you achieve your goals? What can you do to approach Jesus less like Herod and more like a disciple?*

- *When Pilate sarcastically says to Jesus, "What is truth?" he expresses a philosophy of life known as "relativism." What is relativism? In what ways do we see Pilate's relativistic view of life and truth in our culture today?*

- *Because Pilate does not believe in an objective truth—a truth that applies to everyone—he does not have a moral standard outside himself to guide him. He's only left with "his own truth"—the need to protect his own reputation and career, so he sends an innocent man off to be crucified. What are some ways relativism leads to innocent people being hurt in our own culture today?*

Chapter Eleven

SCOURGING, CROWNING, AND THE BARABBAS CHOICE

Jesus is stripped of his garments

The Gospels report how there was a custom of releasing a Jewish prisoner during the Passover feast, so Pilate wants to offer the people Jesus. The chief priests, however, stir up the crowd to ask for another prisoner named "Barabbas."[52]

Who was this Barabbas? The Gospels tell us he was a "notorious" criminal (Matthew 27:16), a revolutionary who had committed murder in a recent uprising in the city (see Mark 15:6-7; Luke 23:18-19). The name Barabbas (*bar abbas*) itself is significant, for it means "son of the father." In the Old Testament,

---

[52] Though many translations of this verse call this prisoner simply "Barabbas," some of the early manuscripts of Matthew's Gospel identify him as "Jesus Barabbas."

Israel was called God's son (Exodus 4:22), and in the Gospels, Jesus calls himself God's Son and the true representative of the people of Israel. But now this other "son of the father" appears and the crowds have to choose between him and Jesus.

When Pilate stands before the crowds with this offer, the people in Jerusalem are faced with one final choice: the rebel Barabbas or Jesus of Nazareth. This is not merely a choice between two prisoners. It is a symbolic choice between two very different men who represent two radically different ways of being Israel, of being "son of the father." One is striving to fight off the Romans with insurrection and murder, while the other calls the Jews to love and forgive their enemies. One represents the way of violent revolution, while the other condemned hatred, violence, and vengeance (see Matthew 5:43-47, 21:4-5, 26:52), and taught instead that the way of mercy, peace, and enduring persecution is what leads to blessing and life (see Matthew 5:7-12, 41-44).

Which one is the true Israelite? Who is the true *bar abbas*—the true Son of the Father?

Ultimately, it comes down to choosing between the way of violent revolution or the way of sacrificial love—the way of the Cross. The crowds will choose the former, foreshadowing how Jerusalem will soon embrace the hopeless way of rebellion against Rome. Meanwhile, Jesus will be sent down the second path—the way of the Cross— modeling the kind of sacrificial love that ushers in the kingdom of God.

The first step for Jesus down that path is what the Catholic Tradition has called the Second Sorrowful Mystery of the Rosary: Pilate sends Jesus to be scourged (see John 19:1).

Scourging at the Pillar

When it comes to matters of legal discipline, the Jews tended to show some restraint. According to the Torah, if a prisoner were to receive a whipping, he could face up to forty lashes, but no more (see Deuteronomy 25:3). Jesus, however, did not face a Jewish whipping. He was sent off for a Roman scourging, which was much more severe and had no limits.

A scourging involved leather thongs with sharp pieces of bones or metal that tore deeply into the skin, leaving skin hanging from the back in bloody strips and sometimes causing muscles and bones to be exposed. The first century Jewish historian Josephus tells of one man being "lacerated to the bone with scourges"[53] and another whose "entrails were visible."[54] The prisoner typically was tied to a post or a pillar and likely stripped for the scourging. There was no limit as to how many times he could be scourged. The punishment caused serious injury, sometimes leaving the prisoner handicapped or dead.

> He may have been half dead before he even picked up his cross.

What was the purpose of scourging? It could be used as a punishment for criminals and as a deterrent for future crimes. It was also used to torture prisoners to get information out of them. Pilate seems to send Jesus for a scourging to make him look so wretched that the Jewish leaders might be satisfied and willing to have him released.

Scourging also was used as a prelude to a crucifixion. One could control the length of a crucifixion by the severity of the scourging. The lighter the scourging, the longer it would take for someone to die during crucifixion; the more intense the scourging, the quicker death would ensue from the cross. Most crucifixions took a day or two to kill a prisoner. The fact that Jesus died in only six hours (see Mark 15:25, 34) tells us he must have had a most horrific scourging. He may have been half dead before he even picked up his cross.

---

[53] Josephus, *War of the Jews,* 6.5.3; #304.
[54] Ibid., 2.612.

Crowning with Thorns

Imagine hundreds of soldiers kneeling before a man wearing a crown and a royal cloak while holding a royal scepter in his hand. The soldiers bow down to pay homage to the king, saying, "Hail, King!" Such a scene seems like the height of royal splendor, recalling how Roman soldiers would bow down before the emperor, saying, "Hail, Caesar!" Here on Good Friday, however, this is the height of humiliation as the soldiers mock him for claiming to be a king.

The Gospels report a whole cohort—which is 600 Roman soldiers—participating in this mocking of Christ. They dress him up like a king. They put a crown on Christ's head, but it is one made of thorns—perhaps from the date palms whose spikes were twelve inches long and were known for causing sharp pain.[55] They put a robe on him that is colored purple, which is the emperor's color and one symbolizing royalty, for the purple dye that came from shellfish was expensive. They put a reed in his right hand, symbolizing a royal scepter (see Matthew 27:27-29).

They bend their knees before Jesus and say, "Hail, King!" mimicking the honoring position of kneeling and the words of praise, "Hail, Caesar!" from soldiers when paying homage to the emperor. But the royal garb and praise are all in jest. And the mockery soon turns violent. As the soldiers come up to Jesus, instead of giving him the kiss of greeting, they strike Jesus, spit on him, and hit him on the head with the reed. In his scourging and crowning with thorns, Jesus fulfills the prophecy: "I gave my back to those who struck me, and my cheeks to those who pulled out the beard; I hid not my face from shame and spitting" (Isaiah 50:6).

The great irony in this scene is that the soldiers will find themselves in the same position of kneeling before Jesus the Lord at the end

---

55 *Midrash Rabbah* on Numbers 3:1; Whitacre, *John*, 447.

of time. For as St. Paul taught, "at the name of Jesus every knee should bow, in heaven, on earth and under the earth" (Philippians 2:10). When they kneel before Jesus at the Last Judgment, they will wish they had not mocked him on Good Friday.

REFLECTION QUESTIONS

- *Barabbas and Jesus represent two very different ways to bring about the kingdom of God and change the world. Barabbas was a revolutionary, someone wanting to use political scheming, plotting, force, and violence to change the social situation of the Jewish people. What does Jesus say is the way to bring about the kingdom?*

- *Following Jesus' teaching and example, what are some of the most important things we should do to extend Christ's kingdom in our workplace, in our parish or ministry, or in our families? In what ways might we be tempted, like Barabbas, to think it's all up to us?*

- *When we consider the intense suffering Jesus endured for our sake in his scourging, it challenges us. Jesus never complains. Meanwhile, we tend to whine over the smallest inconvenience such as traffic, the air conditioner not working, or a coworker not completing a task on-time. How might Jesus' example inspire you to bear the little crosses you face each day with more peace and joy?*

Chapter Twelve

ECCE HOMO:
BEHOLD THE MAN

Ecce Homo by Titian

After having Jesus scourged, Pilate presents him before the crowds, humiliated, wearing a crown of thorns, and the purple robe of royalty. Pilate mockingly says to the crowds, "Behold, the man!" (John 19:5, NAB).

For Pilate, these are words of ridicule but intended to satisfy the crowds and get the people to favor releasing Jesus. It is as if Pilate is saying to them, "Behold, this pitiful man." Having shamed Jesus in this way, Pilate hopes it will be enough for the blood thirsty crowds. After all, what reason can there be for crucifying such a man as this? He may be dressed like a king, but he is clearly no threat to Roman rule. He is only a most pitiable man.

Nevertheless, the careful reader of John's Gospel notices that Pilate is saying more than he realizes. As with other characters in this Gospel, Pilate's words, "Behold, the man," are packed with deeper theological meaning than he himself intends. Pilate says those words to mock Jesus, but in the process, unconsciously points to some important truths about him. Some see Pilate's statement as unwittingly alluding to Jesus as the "son of man" prophesied by Daniel.[56] Others see in Pilate's words an allusion to Jesus as the New Adam (see chapter four), or the Last Adam, who according to St. Paul, became the life-giving spirit and source of resurrection for all the faithful (1 Corinthians 15:45).

The words of Pilate, however, most closely resemble those found in the messianic prophecy of Zechariah 6:12, which uses the expression "Behold the man ..." in reference to the future king, the son of David who "shall bear royal honor" and shall "sit and rule upon his throne."[57]

> Behold the man ... he shall grow up in his place, and he shall build the temple of the LORD. It is he who shall build the temple of the LORD and shall bear royal honor, and shall sit and rule upon his throne. And there shall be a priest by his throne and peaceful understanding shall be between them both. (Zechariah 6:12-13)

Jesus is being mocked for claiming to be a king, but once again we have another instance of an unconscious prophet in Christ's passion pointing to the truth. Pilate says, "Behold the man ..." (John 19:5, NAB) to shame Jesus. But in so doing, the Roman governor unwittingly uses language from the Jewish Scriptures that reveal Jesus is the long-awaited messiah-king whom Zechariah foretold.

---

[56] Jesus himself earlier said in John's Gospel, "When you have lifted up the *son of man*, you will know that I AM" (John 8:28, emphasis added). So now that Jesus is soon to be lifted up on the Cross, Pilate says, "Behold the man," recalling the "son of man" of Daniel 7.

[57] Zechariah 6:12 foretells how the future king will fulfill the prophecies about a royal branch coming out of the stump of Jesse, David's father (Isaiah 11:1-2; Jeremiah 23:5; 33:15). In Zechariah, the word of the Lord says, "*Behold, the man* whose name is the Branch: for he shall grow up in his place, and he shall build the temple of the LORD ... and shall bear royal honor and shall sit and rule upon his throne" (Zechariah 6:12-13, emphasis added).

Pilate's New Fear

Up until this point, the chief priest's charges against Jesus have remained primarily on the political level, making Jesus out to be someone "stirring up the people," forbidding the payment of taxes to Caesar and making himself a king. From their perspective, this was a smart opening move to grab Pilate's attention and get him to act. Now, however, the crowds are demanding Jesus' crucifixion, and Pilate is losing control of the situation, so all the momentum is in their favor. Now they can unveil their underlying religious motive for wanting Jesus killed: "We have a law, and by that law he ought to die, because he has made himself the Son of God" (John 19:7). It is Jesus' claim to be the divine Son of God that irks them the most. And according to Leviticus 24:16, such blasphemy is to be punished with the death penalty.

This sparks a new fear in Pilate: "When Pilate heard these words, he was the more afraid" (John 19:8). On one hand, he realizes now the religious reason for their being so adamant that Jesus be crucified. He doubts he will ever be able to win them over to releasing Jesus. On the other hand, their calling Jesus the Son of God makes Pilate nervous about mishandling the situation. As a gentile, he probably would have understood the title Son of God as a divine man coming with a message from the gods. As a Roman, Pilate would have been familiar with various stories about gods appearing in human form and punishing those who reject them. If Pilate were superstitious enough, the weight of his decision about what to do with Jesus reaches a whole new level: Is Jesus just a failed messiah or is he a deity in disguise? This dilemma makes Pilate take Jesus aside one more time to ask him, "Where are you from?" He is likely wondering if he is from heaven? From the gods? Or just from Galilee?

Jesus remains silent for the third time. He stood silent before the Sanhedrin and before Herod. Now he dares not to speak in front of this man who cares nothing for truth (see John 18:38). He remains quiet before his accusers, fulfilling once again the prophecy of the suffering servant who though oppressed and afflicted, "opened not his mouth" (Isaiah 53:7).

"No Friend of Caesar"

The crowds, on the other hand, have no problem opening their mouths after Pilate makes another attempt to release Jesus. They pull out all the stops and threaten Pilate this time, shouting out, "If you release this man, you are not Caesar's friend; everyone who makes himself a king sets himself against Caesar" (John 19:12).

> It is hard to imagine the chief priests saying something that does more to deny the very faith they claim to be protecting .

In the ancient Greco-Roman world, the title "friend of the king" was given to a special group who were honored by the ruler for their loyalty, given authority and served as trusted advisors.[58] In Rome, too, the emperors were known to bestow "friendship" upon trusted associates. In the early days of the Roman Empire, the "friends of Augustus" were a well-known group. Later in the first century, the emperor Vespasian (AD 69-70) had a group known for their loyalty and authority designated with the title "friend of Caesar."[59] For the crowds to say Pilate is not a "friend of Caesar" is not merely a general accusation that the governor is not loyal to Rome. It is a charge that strikes at the core of his very identity as a Roman governor and status as "friend of the king." The implication is that any Roman leader who harbors or releases a man claiming to be a rival king to Caesar would be guilty of the most severe crime in Rome—treason. Such a man would lose his status as Caesar's friend.

---

[58] 1 Maccabees 2:18; 3:38; 10:65; 3 Maccabees 4:23; Josephus, *Ant.* 12.7.3; #298.

[59] Whitacre, *John*, 457.

All this is more than Pilate can bear. Even though he knew Jesus was an innocent man (see Matthew 27:24) and had declared, "I did not find this man guilty" (Luke 23:14) and "I find no crime in him" (John 18:38), Pilate cannot afford a bad report going to Rome accusing him of releasing a rival king. Even though Pilate knew it was out of envy that the chief priests handed Jesus over to him (see Matthew 27:18), and he had repeatedly tried to release Jesus, too much was at stake for his own career. The pressure reaches its tipping point. Remaining a friend of Caesar is much more important than being a friend to Jesus.

"No King but Caesar" (John 19:14-15)

Now, at last, the chief priests know they have got Pilate where they want him. To seal the deal, they press in and make one more statement that ensures Pilate will not resist their will. When the governor sits on the judgement seat, the crowds cry out, "Away with him, away with him, crucify him!" Pilate sarcastically responds, "Shall I crucify your King?" The chief priests answer, "We have no king but Caesar" (John 19:14-15).

These represent the last words the chief priests speak to Pilate during the trial. They are full of irony. It is hard to imagine the chief priests saying something that does more to deny the very faith they claim to be protecting in their push for Jesus' crucifixion.

In the Jewish law, the people of Israel are to have no foreigner ruling over them (see Deuteronomy 17:15). God alone is king (see Judges 8:23; 1 Samuel 8:4-20), and he rules the people through his appointed Davidic dynasty (see 2 Samuel 7:11-16; Psalm 2:7). The Jewish leaders reaffirm this belief in God's kingship in a prayer they recite every day, "May you be our King, you alone." This was especially at the forefront of their minds during Passover, when they sang, "From everlasting to everlasting you are God; beside you we have no king, redeemer, or savior; no liberator, deliverer, provider, none who takes pity in every time of distress and trouble; we have no king but you."[60] Now, after centuries of waiting for God to come as king and the messiah-king appearing in the person of Jesus Christ, the chief priests declare *Caesar* to be king. Feel the weight of that. The priests who are supposed to be representing the Jewish people choose for their king *not* the God of Israel, *not* the Jewish messiah, *not* the true son of David, but the Roman emperor who is oppressing them.

Washing Hands

Pilate attempts to assuage his conscience and distance himself from the guilt of sending an innocent man to be crucified. He washed his hands before the crowd in a symbolic gesture that would have been quite familiar to the Jews: ritual washing of hands in innocence (see Matthew. 27:24). Pilate's action recalls the Psalms that say, "I wash my hands in innocence" (Psalm 26:6). It also brings to mind the ritual the Torah prescribes for hand washing when someone is killed but the murderer is unknown. According to Deuteronomy 21, the elders where the murder occurred are to sacrifice a heifer and wash their hands and declare, "our hands did not shed this blood" (Deuteronomy 21:7). In a similar vein, Pilate washes his hands and tells the crowd, "I am innocent of this righteous man's blood; see to it yourselves," meaning they need to accept the responsibility for this man's death (Matthew 27:25; see Deuteronomy 21:6-9).

This is something the crowds are wholeheartedly willing to do. They respond, "His blood be on us and on our children!" (Matthew 27:26). They are using a formal statement that is found often in the Old Testament: "x's blood on y." The statement

---

[60] See Whitacre, 456.

expresses responsibility for someone's death.[61] In saying "His blood be upon us and on our children," the crowd accepts the responsibility for Christ's death not only on their own behalf, but on behalf of their family, even to the next generation.

At first glance, it might appear that Pilate has successfully cleared his conscience. After all, he declared Jesus a "righteous man," washed his hands clean of the crucifixion, declared himself innocent of Christ's blood, and got the people to accept responsibility for his death. What more does he need to do? Pilate might go to sleep that night thinking he did everything he could to spare Jesus. But he did not. Pilate's handwashing move, in the end, does not work. He might not want to be associated with responsibility for Jesus' death, but history will not let him get away with that. The truth of his cowardice has been enshrined in human history to this day. Millions of people over the last 2,000 years have continued to remember the truth of what Pilate did on Good Friday every time they recite the Apostle's Creed: "he suffered under Pontius Pilate."

---

[61] See Leviticus 20:9; Deuteronomy 19:10; Joshua 2:19; 2 Samuel 1:16; Ezekiel 18:13, 33:4-6; Acts 5:28, 18:6.

────────── **REFLECTION QUESTIONS** ──────────

- *Pilate was a coward on Good Friday. He was afraid of what people would say about him, so he sent Jesus to be crucified. In what ways might Christians be afraid of what others think of them? How might that fear hinder them from living their faith more fully? How might it keep them from standing up for their faith?*

- *Now let's consider how we might find ourselves like Pilate. Describe a time when you let yourself be controlled by fears about what others will think of you. What do you wish you did differently?*

- *When Pilate condemns Jesus, he immediately feels guilty. But instead of repenting of his action, he washes his hands in a gesture to try to distance himself from Christ's crucifixion and ease his conscience. Do you notice that sense of guilt in you when you do something wrong? What are some ways you sometimes might try to "wash your hands" and silence the voice of your conscience? What should you do instead?*

Chapter Thirteen

CARRYING THE CROSS: SIMON OF CYRENE AND THE WOMEN OF JERUSALEM

Sixth station of the *Via Dolorosa*, Jerusalem, Guiding Star Pilgrimages, LLC

Crucifixions usually took place outside the city walls on crowded roads where many people could see. The point was to send a powerful message: This is what happens if you dare to rise up against Rome!

The vertical part of the cross was implanted at the execution site. On his way there, the prisoner typically carried his own crossbeam over his shoulders like a yoke through the city streets. It would be highly unusual for the Romans to allow another person to carry the crossbeam on behalf of the condemned criminal.

Yet that is exactly what we find in the Gospels. The fact that the Roman soldiers enlisted someone to carry Jesus' cross tells us that Jesus must have received such a severe scourging that he did not have the strength to carry his own crossbeam.[62] The soldiers themselves would not think of carrying it, given the shame linked with such an act. Instead, they press into service a man coming in from the country named Simon of Cyrene to do the job.

Who is this Simon of Cyrene? Mark's Gospel mentions he was the father of Alexander and Rufus. Matthew, Mark, and Luke note he is from the city of Cyrene, which was the capital of the North African district of Cyrenaica. There was a significant Jewish population in the area.[63] Luke, in fact, mentions that devout Jews from the city come to Jerusalem for Jewish feasts (see Acts 2:10), there was a synagogue of Cyrenians (see Acts 6:9), and Christian evangelists eventually come from this city (see Acts 11:20, 13:1). Whether Simon had become a permanent resident in Jerusalem, the Bible does not say. More likely, he was just visiting the city as a pilgrim to celebrate the feast of Passover, like many of his fellow Cyrenians did for other feasts (see Acts 2:10).

How is Simon a model of compassion? He did it out of compulsion! In Luke 23:26, Simon is described as coming from the countryside, which tells us something important. Whoever this Simon is, he was not a part of the riotous crowds demanding Christ's crucifixion at Pilate's praetorium. Coming into the city from the countryside, he suddenly finds himself enveloped by a raucous crowd and forced by Roman soldiers to carry a condemned man's crossbeam.

[62] The word "cross" (*stauros*) can refer to "crossbeam." Brown, *Death of the Messiah,* 2:913. Seneca, *De vita beata* 19.3.

[63] See Acts 2:10; Josephus, *Ag. Ap.* 2:44; *Ant.* 16:160-70; 1 Maccabees 15:23; 2 Maccabees 2:23.

Compassion or Compulsion?

The story of Simon of Cyrene carrying Christ's cross used to puzzle me. Whenever I attended Stations of the Cross as a child, the prayers focused on Simon being a model of compassion. He helped Jesus carry his cross, and we, like Simon, should help others carry their crosses in life. I often wondered, "How is Simon a model of compassion and generous service? He didn't volunteer for this job. He didn't look at Jesus with pity and offer to help. Rather, he was forced to do it. Simon did not carry Christ's cross out of compassion. He did it out of compulsion!"

There is one detail in Luke's account, however, that suggests there is more to the story of Simon of Cyrene than simply carrying the crossbeam of a condemned man. Luke subtly seems to point to how Simon was *transformed* from his unexpected encounter with Christ's cross. For Luke describes Simon as carrying the cross "behind" Jesus (Luke 23:27).

This portrayal of Simon taking Christ's cross and following behind Jesus is a powerful image of discipleship. Consider how Jesus himself taught that one of the most essential criteria for being a disciple is to take up the cross and follow him:

> "If any man would come after me, let him deny himself, *take up his cross and follow me*" (Luke 9:23, emphasis added).

> "Whoever does not bear his own cross and *come after me* cannot be my disciple" (Luke 14:27, emphasis added).

Now consider what Luke tells us about Simon of Cyrene:

> "They laid on him the cross to carry it *behind* Jesus" (Luke 23:26, emphasis added).

What does it look like to be a disciple? To take up the cross and follow Jesus. What does Simon do? He takes Jesus' cross and follows behind him. Luke gives us a powerful visual aid of what discipleship looks like in Simon. In doing so, Luke subtly points to how Simon did not merely help Jesus that day. Simon was changed through his brief encounter with the cross of Christ. Such a quick transformation fits with what Luke's Passion narrative tells of others who encounter Jesus briefly. On Good Friday, Jesus transforms the people we might least expect, and he does not need a lot of time to do it. One of the revolutionaries crucified with Jesus (known as "the good thief"), for example, ends up begging to be remembered by Christ when he enters into his kingdom (see Luke 23:42). The Roman centurion standing under the Cross witnesses Jesus breathe his last breath, and unexpectedly declares, "Certainly this man was innocent!" (Luke 23:47). If these minor characters in the drama of Christ's passion can have a conversion of heart through their brief encounter with Christ, so could Simon.[64]

Luke's account would support the tradition that Simon of Cyrene did not just physically pick up a cross and follow Jesus; he also eventually did so *spiritually* as a disciple, becoming a Christian, as others in his city eventually did (see Acts 11:20, 13:1). Moreover, the way Mark's Gospel mentions that Simon was the father of Alexander and Rufus suggests his sons were well-known believers in the early Church—so well-known they did not need any introduction and were simply mentioned by name (see Mark 15:21). Mark seems to assume his readers know them already. If that connection is true, that might add further biblical support for Simon's transformation after carrying Christ's cross. He became a disciple of Christ, and his children became well-known Christians. Perhaps Simon's son Rufus is the same Rufus that St. Paul mentions in his Letter to the Romans—the only other Rufus in the New Testament and one Paul extols as being "eminent in the Lord" (Romans 16:13). Such an honorable description would be most fitting if this Rufus is the one whose father carried Jesus' cross on Good Friday.

---

[64] See Brown, *Death of the Messiah*, 2:918: "Yet for Luke, contact with Jesus changes people unexpectedly and suddenly."

The Crosses We Do Not Expect

The story of Simon of Cyrene reminds us that it is the crosses we least expect that often bear the most fruit in our lives. Simon was not planning on doing community service hours or volunteering for prison ministry that day. He was not out on the streets looking for condemned men he could help. He was just coming in to the city for the feast of Passover, minding his own business, when suddenly Roman soldiers forced him to carry Christ's cross. This was not on his calendar or to-do list for that day. It was not something he prepared for or anticipated, yet he was transformed through this unexpected cross.

The same is true for us. The crosses we plan are usually easier to embrace than the ones we do not. It is easier to plan our penances ("I'll give up chocolate for Lent"), or volunteer to help when it conveniently fits our schedule. But what about those unexpected crosses that often come our way? A car breaks down. A child breaks down. A friend lets you down. Things do not work out the way you hoped. What do you do in those moments?

It reminds me of something St. Philip Neri once stated: "Never try to evade the cross that God sends you, for you will only find a heavier one."[65] It is not as if God throws crosses at us and wants us to suffer just for the sake of suffering. Because we live in a fallen world, there is going to be suffering in life. None of us can run away from that. When God permits us to face a certain cross, that means he wants us to encounter him there, precisely in the challenge, difficulty, or trial. He does not want us to run away. For if we try to evade the crosses that God allows us to face, we will only find heavier ones because Jesus is not waiting for us in those. Those are crosses we will have to carry more on our own.

If we dare to meet him in the crosses that come our way, we should trust not only that he will give us the grace to carry them,

---

[65] As cited in Bert Ghezzi, *The Voices of the Saints* (New York: Doubleday, 2002), 304.

but also that he can bring good out of them like he did for Simon of Cyrene that day. God can use the unexpected crosses in life to give us the opportunity to grow in some way—to grow in patience, courage, trust, humility, or compassion. Simon ended up receiving a lot more than Christ's cross that day. Through that unexpected cross, he eventually came to experience the fullness of life that comes from following Jesus as a disciple, and his life was changed forever.

Was Jesus Harsh to the Women?

Picture the following scene. The women of Jerusalem are "bewailing and lamenting" Jesus' being sent to be crucified. He sees these compassionate women on the city streets, turns to them, and says these dark, cryptic words:

> Daughters of Jerusalem, do not weep for me, but weep for yourselves and for your children. For behold, the days are coming when they will say, "Blessed are the barren, and the wombs that never bore, and the breasts that never nursed!" Then they will begin to say to the mountains, "Fall on us"; and to the hills, "Cover us." For if they do this when the wood is green, what will happen when it is dry? (Luke 23:28-30)

Have you ever wondered about these words? What does Jesus mean? Of all the things he could discuss with the women on the way to Calvary, why does he speak of wombs never bearing children, mountains falling on people, and green and dry wood?

And do not his words seem harsh? These women are compassionately mourning Jesus' death, and instead of saying, "Thank you ... This means a lot to me," he tells them not to weep for him but for themselves and their children.

Admittedly, from our twenty-first century perspective, Christ's words to the women of Jerusalem seem bewildering. Yet Jesus is using a lot of apocalyptic imagery that his fellow Jews would have been familiar with, because it comes right out of the Jewish Scriptures. Let us look at the context and then unpack the Old Testament background to each of these expressions.

"Daughters of Jerusalem"

That the women are described as "bewailing" and "lamenting" Jesus is significant (Luke 23:27). The word for bewailed (*ekoptesthai*) is used elsewhere in the New Testament to depict someone beating their breasts with grief, such as when those mourning the death of Jairus' daughter beat their breasts (see Luke 8:52; Matthew 11:17). And the word describing the women lamenting (*thrēnoun*) depicts verbal mourning or singing a dirge (see Matthew 11:17; Luke 7:32; John 16:20).[66]

The women's behavior also recalls a prophecy about how Jerusalem would mourn over Christ's death: "The inhabitants of Jerusalem ... when they look on him whom they have pierced, they shall mourn for him, as one mourns for an only child" (Zechariah 12:10-14). Zechariah foretold how the people of Jerusalem would "beat themselves" and "mourn" over the one they pierced. Now, the women of Jerusalem are depicted doing just what Zechariah foretold: beating their breasts and lamenting over Jesus who is about to be crucified.[67] How will Jesus respond?

First, Jesus addresses the women as "daughters of Jerusalem" (Luke 23:28-30), which would bring to mind an important theme in the Jewish prophets: that of the faithful people of God being personified as "daughter of Zion" or "daughter of Jerusalem."[68] In several prophecies, God's suffering people represented by the Daughter of Jerusalem image are called to rejoice, for God is coming to rescue them. Their suffering will turn to rejoicing as God comes to his people as king and liberates them from their enemies.

By calling these women "daughters of Jerusalem," Jesus offers them some hope amid their sorrows. They lament right now that

---

[66] The Jewish historian Josephus, for example, used the same two words to describe the mourning over King Saul's death. *Ant. 6, 14, 8 + 377.* 1 Samuel 31:11-13.

[67] Some scholars reject this interpretation arguing Jesus has not yet been pierced at Calvary. But he already has suffered so much in his passion, having been scourged and pierced by the crown of thorns. And he is now on the way to the site of execution, where he will be pierced in his hands and his feet and then, after his death, in his side (John 19:34).

[68] Isaiah 37:22, 52:2, 62:11; Zephaniah 3:14; Zechariah 9:9.

the Romans are about to crucify him, but that is not the end of the story. Their sorrow will turn to joy when he rises from the dead.

"Do Not Weep"

Second, Jesus wants to redirect their sorrows. He says to them, "Do not weep"—which are the same words he spoke to those who mourned for the widow at Nain whose only son died (see Luke 7:13), and those mourning over the daughter of a man named Jairus who died (see Luke 8:52). In both cases, the mourners did not need to weep because Jesus had come to raise their children from the dead. Now, as he approaches his own death, Jesus tells the women of Jerusalem, "Do not weep for me." Jesus already has demonstrated his power over death. The one who raised the dead in his public ministry can raise himself after his death on the Cross.

Then he says, "Weep for yourselves and for your children" (Luke 23:28). These women with great compassion for Jesus are mourning his approaching death. In response, Jesus seems to reprimand them and say they should instead be weeping for themselves. What do these words mean?

Here, Jesus foretells the suffering the people in Jerusalem will soon face when the city rebels and is destroyed by Rome in AD 70. In fact, this prophecy is built on a series of ominous oracles Jesus gave about the holy city, culminating in two that he gave when he arrived there the week of his death. Let us look at these two oracles, both of which announce the anguish the women of Jerusalem and their children will endure.

When he first drew near to the city, Jesus himself *wept* over Jerusalem and gave a prophecy about the plight of *women and children* caught in city when Rome comes to destroy it:

> Would that even today you knew the things that make for peace! But now they are hidden from your eyes. For the days shall come upon you, when your enemies will cast up a bank about you and surround you, and hem you in on every side,

and dash you into the ground, *you and your children within you*, and they will not leave one stone upon another in you. (Luke 19:41-44, emphasis added)

Jesus knows the future and compassionately weeps over the devastation mothers with children within their wombs will face when Rome dashes them to the ground during their invasion of Jerusalem.

Later that same week, Jesus gave another prophecy about the suffering that women with children will face in that day:

But when you see Jerusalem surrounded by armies, then know that its desolation has come near. Then let those who are in Judea flee to the mountains, and let those who are inside the city depart ... Alas *for those who are with child and for those who are nursing in those days!* (Luke 21:20-23, emphasis added)

Again, Jesus knows all that will unfold in Jerusalem and empathetically laments what Rome will do to the people, even to expecting mothers and those with nursing children.

We see how these earlier prophecies involve the women of Jerusalem and their children. Now, on his way to Calvary, Jesus brings these two themes together again as he tells the "daughters of Jerusalem" to weep not for him, but for themselves and their children. Like the mourners over the widow's son at Nain or those lamenting Jairus' daughter, these women of Jerusalem do not need to weep over Jesus. He lays down his life on his own. He has the power to lay it down and the power to take it again (see John 10:18). Jesus will raise himself from the dead.

Jesus laments, however, that these women soon will have much to weep for in their own lives, as their children's generation will revolt against Rome and pay the price. They come to show compassion over his own plight, but he responds in *compassion for them*, grieving the more severe suffering they will endure. He says to them, "Do not weep for me, but weep for yourselves and for your children" (Luke 23:28).

Blessed Are the Barren?

Jesus' next words to the women of Jerusalem are even more perplexing. He cryptically starts talking about barren women being blessed, people telling mountains to fall on top of them, and green and dry wood.

First, what does Jesus mean by saying, "Blessed are the barren ..." (Luke 23:29)? In Scripture, are not children considered a blessing while barrenness is viewed as a curse? In what sense would Jesus describe barrenness as a blessing? As we have seen, the women in Jerusalem who have children will suffer greatly in watching their children endure the wrath of Rome. When the Roman armies press in on Jerusalem, the barren will be spared untold affliction that those with children will not be able to escape. As one New Testament scholar explains, "Jesus, in a beatitude of bitter irony, declares that the barren are the blessed ones, since children will only bring pain."[69]

Jesus' next words about people saying "to the mountains 'Fall on us'; and to the hills, 'Cover us'" can be seen in a similar light. The words are pleas for a quick death in the face of overwhelming distress. They are taken from a prophecy in the book of Hosea about the destruction of Samaria (see Hosea 10:8). Just as the people of Samaria in the day of their destruction cried out for a quick death, so the inhabitants of Jerusalem will rather die expediently than endure all that Rome will inflict on the city.

Green and Dry Wood

Finally, the green and dry wood imagery should be taken in the same vein. In Scripture, fire is often an image for judgment and punishment (see Isaiah 10:16-19; Jeremiah 11:16; Ezekiel 20:47, 24:9-10). Green wood is not easily burned because it is moist, while dry wood is easier to burn.

---

[69] Robert Tannehill, *Luke* (Nashville: Abingdon Press, 1996), 339.

The point Jesus is making is that if this is how the Romans treat an innocent man like him, how much worse will they treat the people in Jerusalem when the city is in open rebellion against Rome? If innocent, peace-promoting, love-your-enemy Jesus suffers the punishment of a revolutionary, how much more will the real revolutionaries suffer at the hands of Rome? Jesus is saying he is like green wood, and the Jewish revolt movements are like dry wood. You do not usually throw green wood into the fire. If crucifixion is what the Romans do to someone innocent like him (green wood), imagine what they will do with the real Jewish revolutionaries (dry wood). They will burn the city to the ground.

No wonder Jesus tells the women of Jerusalem to weep not for him but for themselves and for their children. Many of their children playing on the streets that Good Friday will be part of the rebellion in AD 70—and they will pay the price.

———————— **REFLECTION QUESTIONS** ————————

- *What is more challenging: the crosses and sacrifices you plan in advance (for example, "I will give up all sweets for Lent" or "I will volunteer at the parish each week this fall") or the ones that come unexpectedly? Why?*

- *Simon did not volunteer to carry Jesus' cross. He was forced to do so. Yet we saw how he was transformed through his brief encounter with Christ—something good came out of this unexpected cross. How might his example encourage us in our own unexpected crosses? How should we respond when we suddenly face a new trial or suffering?*

- *St. Philip Neri once said, "Never try to evade the cross God sends you, for you will only find a heavier one." What do you think that means? And how might these words encourage you the next time you face an unexpected cross?*

Chapter Fourteen

THE SHORT CRUCIFIXION

The Crucifixion

Crucifixion did not damage any vital organs, but this was no act of mercy. It was more torturous to die slowly, sometimes over a few days while the weight of the unsupported body gradually would cause the breathing muscles to give out. The person would eventually die of shock or asphyxiation. The fact that Jesus' crucifixion was a shorter one—only six hours (see Mark 15:25, 34)—tells us he must have endured a most horrendous scourging. Jesus already may have been on the brink of death by the time he arrived at Calvary.

In Roman crucifixions, the criminal was nailed or bound to the cross with his arms extended and raised. Not being able to move, he was unable to cope with cold, heat, pain, insects, or animals that might bother him. The fact that John's Gospel later tells us about the prints of nails in Jesus' hands indicates that Jesus was not tied to the cross but nailed to it (see John 20:25; Luke 24:39).

Some criminals were attached only on the vertical stake that stood at the execution site. More often, however, the prisoner would do what Jesus was initially forced to do: carry a crossbeam to the place of execution. There, the crossbeam would be attached either to the *top* of the stake (making the cross T-shaped), or in a notch just below the top of the vertical pole (giving the cross the familiar shape found in Christian symbolism). Which kind of cross did Jesus have on Good Friday? The Bible does not say explicitly, but it does offer an important clue. The fact that the inscription, "This is Jesus, the King of the Jews," was placed *above* Jesus' head (Matthew 27:37), indicates that the crossbeam did not rest *on top* of the vertical stake (as in the T-shape) since there must have been room for the inscription to be nailed above him. That is why we can have confidence that the traditional Christian depiction of Christ's cross is most accurate.

Refusing Wine

What is the name of the place where Jesus died? Many Christians might answer, "Calvary." But did you know the word Calvary is not in Scripture? Still, Calvary is a most appropriate name because it is derived from the Latin word (*calvaria*) for "skull," which is the biblical name given for the place of Jesus' death. The Gospels tell us Jesus is crucified at a site called "Golgotha," which means "place of the skull" (Matthew 27:33). The location may have been called "skull" because it was a place of death or because it describes the rounded knoll's skull-like appearance.

When Jesus arrives at Golgotha, the soldiers do three things as they crucify him. First, they offer him "wine mingled with myrrh" (Mark 15:23). This is the first of two wine offerings that will be given to Jesus.

What is the purpose of this drink? Myrrh had narcotic qualities that would dull pain and induce sleep, and this offering of wine mingled with myrrh reflects the traditional practice of offering a dying person alcohol to ease the pain. As the book of Proverbs teaches, "Give strong drink to him who is perishing, and wine to those in bitter distress; let them drink and forget their poverty and remember their misery no more" (Proverbs 31:6-7).[70]

Why does Jesus refuse this first offering of wine? Probably because he is determined to give himself completely on the Cross, to enter fully into his sacrifice, to drink the last drop from the cup of his suffering. He also wants to remain alert to the end, for he will continue to minister on the Cross, teaching the people, fulfilling prophecy, forgiving sins, and drawing souls to conversion. His refusing this initial offer of wine should not surprise us, for at the Last Supper, he describes his commitment not to drink "the fruit of the vine" until he enters the kingdom: "I shall not drink again of this fruit of the vine until that day when I drink it new with you in my Father's kingdom" (Matthew 26:29).

Clothes Divided

The second thing the soldiers do when they arrive at Calvary is divide Jesus' garments among them by casting lots. Men were typically crucified naked to add to their shame, and the executioners were entitled to whatever remaining items the victim possessed. All four Gospels mention how the soldiers cast lots to divide Christ's garments.

Casting lots was a game of chance, perhaps involving the throwing of dice which the bored soldiers might have had on

---

[70] Matthew mentions the soldiers adding gall to the wine (Matthew 26:34). Gall was a biter substance emanating from the liver into the gall bladder. Its severe bitterness led to the word "gall" being used to describe bitter vegetable substances such as "wormwood" and could even describe poison. What exactly was mixed in to this wine is not clear, but it's possible this "gall," like the myrrh, was intended to dull pain. In any case, whether or not Matthew's original audience would have associated the gall with pain-killing effects, "they would expect the wine itself to serve in a pain-killing function (Proverbs 31:6-7)." Keener, *A Commentary on the Gospel of Matthew,* 678.

hand or guessing the number of hidden fingers an opponent had stretched out. Whatever the specifics of the game may have been, the Gospels mention the divided garments and casting lots to make the first of several allusions to what could be called "the Passion Psalm"—Psalm 22—which features a righteous man who is suffering at the hands of his persecutors. Consider how the details of just a few lines in this Psalm written centuries before Christ foreshadow the suffering he endures when he first arrives at Golgotha:

> Yes, dogs are round about me; a company of evil doers encircle me; they have pierced my hands and feet—I can count all my bones—they stare and gloat over me; they divide my garments among them, and for my clothing they cast lots. (Psalm 22:16-18)

This is exactly what happens to Jesus when he gets to Golgotha. We can see the connections in three ways: First, Jesus' *hands and feet are pierced* as the soldiers crucify him (see John 20:25; Luke 24:39), just as Psalm 22 foretold. Second, the soldiers *"divided his garments among them by casting lots"*—which is the same thing that happened with the suffering righteous man's garments. Then, the soldiers sat and "kept watch over him" (Matthew 27:36), just as Psalm 22 foreshadowed: "they stare and gloat over me." These are just the first of many allusions to Psalm 22 we will find in the Gospel accounts of Christ's crucifixion.

Seamless Tunic

John's Gospel mentions that Christ's garments were divided into four parts, "one for each soldier," indicating there were four soldiers at Calvary, which is the number typically dispatched for crucifixions.[71] But John mentions another clothing item: a tunic

---

[71] "The Roman army's basic unit was a *contubernium*, eight men who shared a tent; normally half of such a unit would be dispatched for a work detail like a crucifixion." Craig Keener, *A Commentary on the Gospel of Matthew* (Grand Rapids, MI: Eerdmans, 1999), 679-680.

that was "without seam, woven from top to bottom." The soldiers decided not to tear this item, but casted lots to determine which soldier would get it (John 19:23-24). It was the third action they performed after they arrived at Calvary.

There is profound symbolism in this "seamless tunic" that was not torn in pieces by the soldiers. On one hand, it recalls the garments the high priest wore. The word for tunic in John 19:23 is "*chitōn*" in Greek, which describes a long inner garment worn next to the skin. It is sometimes used in the Old Testament to refer to one of the high priest's vestments (see Exodus 28:4; Leviticus 16:4), which according to the Law was never to be torn (see Leviticus 21:10), and which the Jewish historian Josephus reports was seamless.[72]

This is why some Church Fathers saw the soldier's decision not to tear the tunic as an allusion to Leviticus 21:10's description of how the high priest's vestments were not to be rent. By drawing attention to this seamless tunic, John's Gospel is trying to show us that on the Cross, Jesus is the true High Priest, wearing a high priest's garment. Unlike Caiaphas who rent his garments, Jesus' tunic is not torn—not by himself or even by the soldiers below. The point is that Jesus is the true High Priest of Israel. And he is far from a passive victim nailed to the Cross. He is the High Priest actively offering the highest sacrifice ever offered to God: the sacrifice of his own life.

On the other hand, a number of Church Fathers saw these two items—the garments divided into four pieces and the one seamless tunic—as symbolizing the division in the human family and the unity of the Church. The early third century bishop St. Cyprian of Carthage, for example, interpreted the four garments as pointing to the four corners of the earth,

---

[72] Josephus describes an ankle-length tunic that was one long woven cloth, not composed of two pieces. *Ant. 3.7.4; 161.*

while the one seamless tunic represents the undivided Church. Cyprian also notes how the tunic being woven "from top to bottom" (John 19:23) adds to the symbolism. Just as the unity of the tunic came from top to bottom and was not torn apart by the soldiers, so the unity of the Church came from on high from God and cannot be divided by men.[73]

There is rich biblical support for this symbolism, both in terms of unity and in terms of division. Of all the Gospels, John emphasizes the theme of unity the most. Jesus himself teaches that his followers are to be "one flock" under "one shepherd" (John 10:16). At the Last Supper, he prays for them that "they may all be one" even as he is one with the Father (John 17:21-22). John's Gospel even states that one of the main purposes of Jesus' death at Golgotha is "to gather into one" the dispersed children of God (John 11:52). He says that he will "draw all men to myself" when he is lifted up on the Cross (John 12:32). So, when we arrive at the place where Jesus will die, it is not surprising that John's Gospel brings the theme of unity to the forefront with the symbol of the seamless tunic presented in contrast with the garments divided into four parts.[74]

There is also strong biblical background to the theme of division in this scene. The soldiers' tearing Christ's garments (*himatia*) into four parts recalls a powerful symbolic action in the Old Testament that signified a dramatic rupture in God's people. In the book of 1 Kings, the prophet Ahijah tore a new garment (*himation*) into twelve pieces to symbolize the tragic division of the kingdom of David and Solomon. The unity of the twelve tribes in the one kingdom soon would be torn apart

---

[73]   Raymond Brown, *The Gospel According to John XII-XXI*, 921.

[74]   In fact, the word John uses to describe the soldiers tearing (*schizein*) Christ's garments is related to the word John often uses to describe the division (*schisma*) among God's people over whether to accept Jesus and his teachings (John 7:43, 9:16, 10:19). For John, the soldiers dividing (*schizein*) the garments, therefore, symbolizes the division (*schisma*) among those who misunderstand and reject Christ.

(see 1 Kings 11:30). Here, the tearing of the *himatia* clearly symbolizes the breakup of God's people. This background also sheds light on Jesus' divided garments at Calvary. The tearing of Christ's garments into four parts represents the division of the human family apart from Christ, scattered across the four corners of the world. Like Solomon's divided kingdom, humanity apart from Jesus is divided and its glory will fade. The one seamless tunic, however, represents the unity of the Church. It cannot be torn apart, and it will endure forever.

The Title: INRI

Have you ever noticed the four capital letters INRI on the crucifixes in some churches? What is their meaning? The letters INRI are an abbreviation for the four Latin words that Pontius Pilate had posted on the cross above Jesus' head: *"Iesus Nazarenus Rex Iudaeorum,"* meaning, "Jesus of Nazareth, the King of the Jews" (John 19:19). Let us now consider the rich significance of this inscription.

All four Gospel accounts tell how an inscription with the charges against Jesus was posted on the Cross, an action for which there is some precedent in ancient Rome. We know that with some crucifixions, the charges were written on a small tablet and when the criminal made his way to the execution site, the tablet was carried before him or worn around his neck.[75] Sometimes those charges could be posted to the cross at the crucifixion itself.[76] If one of the goals of crucifixion is deterring crime, then showcasing the condemned man's offense on his way to execution would be useful and would add to his public shaming.

Christ's plaque reads, "This is Jesus the King of the Jews" and is placed on the cross "over his head"—revealing the ironic truth

---

[75] Brown, *Death of the Messiah,* 2:963; Keener, *The Gospel of John,* 1137.

[76] Keener, *The Gospel of John,* 1137.

of the scene (Mattthew 27:37; see also Luke 23:38). The tablet is intended to mock Jesus, for how can this humiliated, rejected, scourged, and crucified man really be a king? Yet the sign really does point to the truth. Jesus *is* the true King—and not just the king of the Jews. John's Gospel notes how the inscription was written in three languages: Hebrew, Greek, and Latin,

> **Pilate's sign unwittingly reveals that the crucified Jesus is, indeed, the King.**

symbolizing the universality of Christ's kingship. *Hebrew* is the language of the Jewish people, *Latin* is the language of Rome, and *Greek* was the main commercial language of the eastern Mediterranean world.[77] The tri-lingual inscription on the Cross, therefore, reveals Jesus to be not only King of the Jews, but King of the whole world![78]

With this background, we can appreciate more what John's Gospel is trying to emphasize. Jesus is not merely a crucified man; he is the King of the world. The Cross is not merely an instrument of execution; it is Christ's throne. And his death is not his moment of defeat, but the way he wins his kingdom. Through being lifted up on the Cross, Jesus will gather all men to himself (see John 12:32).

Not everyone is impressed by this inscription. The chief priests want it taken down. It is here in John's account that we learn Pilate was the one who wrote the inscription. The chief priests turn to Pilate, asking for it to be rewritten: "Do not write, 'The King of the Jews' but 'This man said, I am the King of the Jews'" (John 19:21).

Pilate, however, refuses to make any changes. He replies, "What I have written, I have written" (John 19:22). Some might say these

---

[77] And in John's Gospel, the Greek brings to mind the Gentiles who are called "Greeks" (John 12:20).

[78] Earlier in John, Jesus himself foretold that it would be precisely when he is "lifted up" on the cross that he would "draw all men to myself" (John 12:32). Now, that climactic moment has arrived at Calvary as Jesus draws all men to himself through the Cross. The universal nature of his mission is hinted at through the inscription in three languages.

words imply no more than a simple denial of the chief priests' request. But Pilate's word for "written" may be significant. For every other time the word "written" has been used in John's Gospel up to this point, it refers to Scripture.[79] The word always comes in the context when a matter of truth from Scripture is being revealed, either in reference to biblical prophecy being fulfilled or Scripture being referred to as an authoritative source for God's law or for telling the great things God has done in biblical history. So, when John's Gospel reports Pilate saying, "What I have written, I have written," it may subtly be showing even further how Pilate's inscription unwittingly reveals the truth—the fulfillment of God's plan, the fulfillment of all that is *written* in Scripture. Jesus really is the King.

Mocking at the Cross

Finally, Matthew tells how three groups of people begin mocking Jesus while he is on the Cross: the people passing by, the chief priests, and the two criminals crucified with Jesus. There are two key themes to consider in this scene that make clear how these final mockeries of Christ are not random acts of meanness but a part of the devil's final assault and a part of God's own plan of salvation.

First, these mockeries were prophetically foreshadowed in Psalm 22—a Psalm that we have already seen come to the forefront in Christ's passion. Recall how this psalm presents a righteous man who is persecuted by his enemies in a way that prefigures what happens when Jesus arrives at Golgotha: the man is pierced in his hands and feet and his persecutors cast lots for his garments. Now, we will see that the way the man's enemies revile him foreshadows the vehement ridicule Jesus faces on the Cross.

Matthew's Gospel tells how the people passing on the road are described as "wagging their heads" (Matthew 27:39). That is not a

---

[79] John 2:17, 6:31, 45, 8:17, 10:34, 12:14, 16, 15:25. See Keener, *The Gospel of John*, 1138.

small background detail but another crucial allusion to Psalm 22. There, the persecuted righteous man says, "All who seek me mock at me, they make mouths at me, *they wag their heads*" (Psalm 22:7, emphasis added). Those passing by Calvary do the exact same thing: they deride Jesus and wag their heads at him, just as Psalm 22 foreshadowed.

Another connection to Psalm 22 comes with the next group of people deriding Jesus. The chief priests, scribes, and elders say, "He trusts in God; let God deliver him now, if he desires him" (Matthew 27:43). Like the wagging of heads, these cruel words also harken back to Psalm 22:8 where the righteous man's enemies say, "*He committed his cause to the LORD; let him deliver him, let him rescue him, for he delights in him!*" Once again, the mocking of the righteous man in Psalm 22 foreshadows what happens to Jesus on the Cross. And notice the irony: precisely in their mocking of Jesus, the ones who reject Jesus unwittingly reveal him to be fulfilling biblical prophecy as they wag their heads and shame him with the words from Psalm 22.

A second important theme in this scene is how all three groups attack Jesus for being the Son of God. First, the people passing by start it off by saying, "If you are the Son of God, come down from the cross" (Matthew 27:40). Let us take a closer look at these opening words: "If you are the Son of God ... " Do you remember who else spoke those exact same opening words to Jesus? Who was it that met Jesus and said to him, "If you are the Son of God ... "? It was the devil. When the devil tempted Jesus in the desert, he said, "*If you are the Son of God*, command these stones to become loaves of bread" (Matthew 4:3, emphasis added). The people passing by are not just speaking cruelties to Jesus. They are echoing the words of the one who hates Christ and who has been opposing him from the very beginning: Satan.

That is not all. The chief priests, scribes, and elders also ridicule Jesus for his claim to divine sonship, saying, "He trusts in God; let God deliver him now, if he desires him, for he said, 'I am the Son of God'" (Matthew 27:39). The men crucified with Jesus mocked him in a similar way (see Matthew 27:44). Notice how all three groups—those passing by, the Jewish leaders, and the other criminals—attack Jesus' identity as the Son of God. The derision of all three groups are not random acts of cruelty. They echo a much darker voice, the voice of the one ultimately behind the attacks on Christ this day—the devil.

───────── REFLECTION QUESTIONS ─────────

- *Christ's kingship challenges us to ask a personal question: Who is the true king in your life? Is it really Jesus? Or is it yourself? Do you wake up each day asking Jesus to guide all your decisions and actions, to help you do his will for your life? Or do you meander through life pursuing your own goals, dreams, plans, and to-do list each day?*

- *What can you do practically to make Jesus not just a part of your life, but the very center? How can you allow him to reign as king on the throne of your heart?*

- *Consider the following prayer from St. Ignatius of Loyola. It's a prayer of surrender, entrusting one's entire life to the Lord Jesus, the King:*

"Take, Lord, and receive all my liberty,
my memory, my understanding, and my entire will,
all that I have and possess.
Thou hast given all to me.
To Thee, O Lord, I return it.
All is thine; dispose of it wholly according to thy will.
Give me Thy love and Thy grace,
for this is sufficient for me."[80]

What part of this prayer is hardest for you? Why? Ask for the grace to say this part with all your heart.

---

[80] St. Ignatius of Loyola, *Spiritual Exercises*, trans. Louis J. Puhl (Chicago: Loyola University Press, 1951), 192.

Chapter Fifteen

DEATH OF
THE MESSIAH

Church of the Holy Sepulchre, Jerusalem

Several cataclysmic events unfold in the moments surrounding Jesus' death—a great darkness, an earthquake, rocks splitting, and the temple veil suddenly torn in two. These, we will see, are *dark apocalyptic signs,* many of which were foreshadowed in the Old Testament and point to God's judgment on the world.

There are also several *prophetic signs of hope*—small, seemingly insignificant details in the Gospel accounts that are packed with deep significance from the Jewish Scriptures. The bones of Jesus are not broken. His body is pierced. Blood and water flow from his side. Tombs open. A rich man and a teacher anoint Christ's body before burying it in a garden tomb.

Every little detail in the Gospel accounts of Christ's death is there for a reason. Every point is charged with great meaning. Many of

147

us miss the significance of the details because we do not know the Old Testament background. As we turn to this climactic moment in Scripture, we will walk step-by-step through these details and unpack the crucial background. While we will discuss in the next chapter each of Jesus' last words (such as "I Thirst" and "It is finished"), here we will focus on both the darkness and light, the many signs of judgment and signs of hope found in the moments surrounding Christ's death.

Darkness and Earthquake

When Jesus died, the land had been covered in darkness for three hours since noon, and at the moment of his death, the earth shook and rocks split (see Matthew 27:45, 51). It is as if the earth itself is groaning over the death of the Son of God. Each of these extraordinary events is an apocalyptic sign foreshadowed in the Old Testament. In Scripture, the earth shaking expresses God's judgment (see Jeremiah 4:24; Joel 2:10) and it is an image Jesus himself used when announcing judgment on Jerusalem (see Mathew 24:7-8). Similarly, Matthew's mention of the rocks being "split" (Matthew 27:51) recalls the prophecy of Nahum that when God's wrath is unleashed, the rocks "are broken asunder by him" (Nahum 1:5-6).

Perhaps the image with the most significance is the darkness covering the whole land from the sixth hour (noon) until Jesus' death at the ninth hour (3 PM) (see Matthew 27:45). This unnatural *three* hours of darkness in the middle of the day would have been viewed as a visible illustration of God's anger. It recalls how a thick *three* days of darkness covered "all the land of Egypt" in the ninth plague before the Passover (Exodus 10:22). Just as God punished Pharaoh for his hard-heartedness in refusing to let his people go, so God is unhappy with the hard-heartedness of the people who have rejected and killed his Son on Good Friday. In this way, the chief priests, scribes, and

Pharisees who plotted against Christ are like the chief enemy of God's people in the book of Exodus: Pharaoh.

Even more, the darkness brings to fulfillment the details of a prophecy of judgment in the book of Amos, chapter eight. God says, "I will make the sun go down at noon and darken the earth in broad daylight" and goes on to describe how he will "turn your feasts into mourning … I will make it like the mourning for an only son" (Amos 8:9-10). All this—the darkness at noon, the feast turning to mourning, and the sorrow over an only son—anticipates what happens on Good Friday. Just as Amos prophesied centuries before Christ, *darkness* descends on Jerusalem at noon around the time of the feast of Passover, which will become a time for mourning—*mourning for God's only Son.*[81]

The Roman Centurion

Not all was death, judgment, and divine displeasure. God also gave several signs of hope—hope that Jesus' death was part of a larger purpose that would bring blessing to the whole world.

One of those signs of hope comes from a most unexpected source—the last person you might expect to suddenly come to faith. The Roman centurion standing at Calvary says, "Truly this man was the Son of God" (Mark 15:39).

Think about who this man is. First, he is not a Jew, but a gentile. Second, he is not any ordinary gentile, but a Roman—a citizen of the empire that was persecuting God's people in Jesus' day. Third, he is no ordinary Roman, but a Roman *centurion*—an officer in charge of one-hundred soldiers. In other words, this particular Roman is one of the leaders carrying out the oppression of the Jewish people.

It is hard to imagine someone at Calvary more unlikely to come to believe in Jesus. Yet this Roman centurion sees what the chief

---

[81] See also Zechariah 1:15; Joel 2:2, 3:4.

priests, Pilate, Herod, and the crowds fail to see that day—that Jesus "truly is the Son of God." The centurion, in fact, echoes what the Father said at Christ's baptism. When Jesus came up from the Jordan River at his baptism, the heavenly voice said, "You are my beloved Son" (Mark 1:11). As such, the centurion's words stand in stark contrast to what the others at the Cross say about Jesus. The chief priests, other criminals, and those passing by *mock* Jesus' sonship, saying, "If you are the Son of God, come down from the cross"(Matthew 27:40). We saw how their mocking of Christ's sonship *echoes the voice of Satan* who tempted Jesus in the desert with similar words, "If you are the Son of God … " (Matthew 4:3). The centurion, however, does just the opposite. He *echoes the Father's voice* at Christ's baptism and confidently affirms Christ's sonship, saying, "Truly this is the son of God."

The Temple Veil

A second sign of hope is found in an ominous event that took place in the Temple right when Jesus died: "the curtain of the temple was torn in two, from top to bottom" (Mark 15:38).[82]

The curtain is torn "from top to bottom," symbolizing how it is a divine act. God is the one who tears open the temple veil. Such an act expresses God's judgment on the Temple and the end to the sacrifices that took place there. The whole temple system of animal sacrifice is no longer needed, for the one perfect sacrifice has now been offered—the sacrifice of Christ.

At the same time, the tearing of the temple veil also points to something beautiful. It reveals a new intimacy with God's presence opening to the human family. Previously, God's presence had dwelt in the innermost chamber of the Temple known as the Holy of Holies, which no ordinary Jew could

---

[82] This curtain refers either to the outer curtain separating the sanctuary from the outer courts or the inner veil that covered the Holy of Holies. Exodus 26:31-5; Levititcus 16:2; 2 Chronicles 3:19.

enter. Only the high priest could enter this sacred space and even he, only once a year. Now, God tears open the temple curtain symbolizing a new access to closeness with him. As a result of Christ's sacrifice for our sins, the path is now being opened for us to draw intimately near to God's holy

> The tearing of the temple veil reveals a new intimacy with God's presence.

presence. As Pope Benedict XVI once explained, God's face in Scripture symbolizes God's presence. When the temple veil is torn, it's as if God is removing his veil so that we can draw near to him and see his face. "Previously, God's face had been concealed ... Now, God himself has removed the veil and revealed himself in the crucified Jesus as the one who loves to the point of death. The pathway to God is open."[83]

Tearing Open

There is even more. Marks' Gospel gives an important detail about this scene that underscores how the temple veil being torn is a climactic moment not only in Christ's passion, but in the entire history of Israel. The word Mark uses here at the end of his Gospel to describe the temple veil being "torn" is *schizo*, which is significant, because Mark used this same word at the beginning of his Gospel when telling about Jesus' baptism:

> And when he came up out of the water, immediately he saw the heavens opened (*schizo*) and the Spirit descending upon him like a dove; and a voice came from heaven, "You are my beloved Son; with you I am well pleased." (Mark 1:10-11)

The word *schizo* itself is an intense, graphic one, meaning to tear open or rend open. The idea of the heavens being torn open at Christ's baptism recalls a prophecy in Isaiah chapter 64. In the oracle, Isaiah is begging God to *tear open the heavens* and come

---

[83] Benedict XVI, *Jesus of Nazareth: Holy Week,* 209.

down to act decisively. He pleads with God to descend from heaven and rescue his people from their enemies:

> O that you would tear the heavens and come down, that the mountains might quake at your presence ... to make your name known to your adversaries and that the nations might tremble at your presence! (Isaiah 64:1-2)

Notice what Isaiah prayed for. He prayed for the day when the *heavens* would be *torn open* and God would come down to rescue the people. When Mark tells how the "heavens" are "torn open" at Christ's baptism, he is announcing that this great day of Isaiah 64 is finally dawning. Isaiah's prayer is starting to be answered. The God of Heaven is descending to earth to liberate Israel from their enemies!

The important detail I want us to notice is how Mark links the heavens being *torn open* at Christ's baptism with the affirmation of his *divine sonship*. When the heavens are torn open that day, the heavenly Father's voice says, "You are *my beloved Son*" (Mark 1:11, emphasis added).

This is important because Mark links these same two themes at one other point in his Gospel: Christ's death on the Cross. Right when Jesus breathes his last, the temple curtain is suddenly "*torn* open" (*schizo*) and the Roman centurion out of nowhere affirms Christ's divine sonship, saying, "Truly this man was the *Son of God!*" (Mark 15:38-39, emphasis added).

By bringing together these two themes at the Cross, Mark shows us that Christ's ministry ends where it began: with the hope of Isaiah for God to come down and save his people. Indeed, that hope which was initially sparked at Christ's baptism is now fulfilled on Calvary. Mark, therefore, is emphasizing that the death of Jesus is not his defeat. It is the decisive moment when Isaiah's plea is finally answered. God has come down and saved his people. The temple veil is *torn* open (*schizo*), giving humanity new access to God's presence through the one whom the centurion has revealed is truly "the *Son of God*."

Pierced, but Not Broken

Sometimes the Romans broke the crucified man's legs with a hammer to prevent the victims from pushing up to catch a breath. This would quickly bring the crucifixion process to its intended outcome causing the victims to die from suffocation within minutes. This is what the Jews asked Pilate to do in order to speed up the process that day, so that the criminals' bodies could be removed before the sabbath starts at sundown (see John 19:31). The soldiers carried out their duty, breaking the bones of the other crucified men, but when seeing Jesus was already dead, they did not break his bones (see John 19:32-33).

Why do we need to know about the unbroken bones? This small point has great biblical significance. As we will discuss more below, it recalls how the Passover lamb was not to have its bones broken (see Exodus 12:46; Numbers 9:12). Jesus dies like an unblemished Passover lamb offered in sacrifice. Christ's unbroken bones also present him as the righteous king in Psalm 34, who would be afflicted by his enemies but be rescued by God. In the end, he would keep all his bones, "not one of them is broken" (Psalm 34:20).

Instead of breaking the legs, a soldier pierces Jesus' side to make sure he was dead (see John 19:34). This small detail is also charged with great significance. It recalls what the prophet Simeon foretold when Mary and Joseph presented the Christ child at the Temple: Jesus one day would have a sword pass through him (see Luke 2:35). It also fulfills a prophecy from Zechariah about how God will send a spirit of compassion and supplication on the inhabitants of Jerusalem "when they look on him *whom they have pierced*" (Zechariah 12:10, emphasis added). We see once again that centuries before Christ, God prophesied what would happen on Good Friday as the people at Calvary look upon Jesus' body which has been pierced by the spear.

Blood and Water

John notes how something happened right when the soldier pierced Christ's side: "At once there came out blood and water" (John 19:34). The fact that *blood* and *water* flow from Christ's side also has important symbolism.

First, the flow of *blood* from Christ's side brings to mind the ancient Jewish sacrifices. According to the prescribed rituals, the blood of the sacrificed animal should flow out at the moment of death so that it could be sprinkled before it congeals.[84] By noting the blood coming forth from Christ's side, John's Gospel underscores how Jesus' death is not merely an execution. It is ultimately a gift to God—a sacrificial offering to the Father. Jesus is offering himself like an animal sacrifice in the temple, a sacrificial victim offered for all humanity. The Cross, therefore, is not just an instrument of death. It is an altar for the greatest act of worship the world has ever known: Christ's perfect offering of himself to the Father.

Second, what is the meaning of the flow of *water*? The image recalls the vision given to the prophet Ezekiel about water pouring forth like a river from the temple, giving life, healing, and forgiveness of sins to all who draw near (see Ezekiel 47). It also brings to mind what Jesus said in his public ministry about how "out of his heart shall flow rivers of living water"—which, as John's Gospel explains, refers to the Spirit that will be given when Christ is glorified on Calvary (John 7:38-39).

When John notes that water flows from Christ's side at his death, he is not just offering an interesting medical observation. He is signaling that Ezekiel 47's life-giving waters flowing from the temple are now being unleashed from the new house of God's presence, the temple of Christ's body (see John 2:19-21). Now

---

84 Mishnah Pesahim 5:3, 5. See Brown, *The Gospel According to John XIII-XXI*, 951.

that Jesus has offered the perfect sacrifice on the Cross, the living water of the Spirit can flow from his pierced heart, just as he had foretold. And it will bring us healing, forgiveness, and new life, just as Ezekiel prophesied.

In sum, the two symbols of blood and water come together to reveal the beauty of what Jesus is accomplishing on the Cross. From the *blood* of Christ's sacrifice on the Cross, comes forth the living *water* of Christ's Spirit to give us new life.

Baptism, Eucharist, and Eve

We have seen a lot of rich biblical symbolism in just these two short verses: the unbroken bones, the pierced side, the water, and the blood. Many Church Fathers saw something more. The water and the blood also symbolize two foundational sacraments: baptism and the Eucharist.

It is important to note that this sacramental interpretation is not a forced one. It is not about Catholics eagerly wanting to see their sacraments in every reference to water and blood in the Bible. The connection between these sacraments and the Cross is actually grounded in John's theology. It is *John's Gospel* that makes this connection, for John himself uses *water* in association with baptism (see John 3:5) and *blood* as an image for the Eucharist (see John 6:53-56). Catholics throughout the centuries have simply picked up on the sacramental connections John himself is making.

One last thought on this verse is to notice how the water and blood flow from the pierced "side" of Christ. This small detail recalls an important scene in the Garden of Eden. We have seen how Jesus in his passion is revealed as a New Adam—taking on the curses of Adam and being obedient to the Father's will where Adam was disobedient. Here, one more connection can be made. Do you recall who came from the side of Adam? His bride, Eve (see Genesis 2:21-22). The water and blood coming from the *side* of the deceased Christ brings to mind Eve coming from the side of the sleeping Adam.

One can understand why many Church Fathers saw in this detail the gifts of baptism and the Eucharist flowing from the pierced side of Jesus, giving birth to the Church and renewing it in every age. Benedict XVI explained, "The opened side of the Lord asleep on the Cross prompted the Fathers to point to the creation of Eve from the side of the sleeping Adam, and so in this outpouring of the sacraments, they also recognized the birth of the Church: the creation of the new woman from the side of the New Adam."[85]

The New Passover Lamb

In his account of Jesus' death, John mentions Christ's last drink, last words, and last breath. He also highlights the fulfillment of prophecy: soldiers casting lots for Jesus' garments, the soldiers piercing Jesus' side, and the blood and water coming out. We have seen how every detail, every word, in these verses is packed with great meaning.

There is, however, one small matter he discusses that still seems quite out of place. At this climactic moment in the history of the world, John suddenly feels the need to talk about a kind of plant: hyssop.

> "So they put a sponge full of vinegar on hyssop and held it to his mouth" (John 19:29).

Of all the details John could tell us about the final moments of Jesus' life, why do we need to know that the plant they used to bring him his last drink was *hyssop*? Surely, there cannot be deep theological meaning in the name of a simple plant? We as readers want to know about more interesting matters: What was Jesus thinking in his dying moments? Did Mary say anything

---

[85] Benedict XVI, *Jesus of Nazareth: Holy Week*, 226.

to her Son before he died? Where were the apostles? Did Pilate have any second thoughts? These would be far more exciting topics than John's botany reference here. At the moments just before Jesus dies, who cares about hyssop!

That is how many modern readers might be tempted to read John's account of this scene. Those familiar with the Jewish Scriptures, like the ancient Jews in Jesus' day, would pick up on the profound point John is making. The simple mention of the hyssop in the context of a Passover feast would recall the first Passover in Egypt—that foundational event in their nationhood when they were liberated from slavery in Egypt. On that first Passover, God instructed the Israelites to sacrifice a lamb, eat the lamb, and put the blood of the lamb on their doorposts so that the angel of death would pass over their homes and spare their families from the tenth plague in Egypt, which brought death to all the firstborn in the land.

> "The opened side of the Lord asleep on the Cross prompted the Fathers to point to the creation of Eve from the side of the sleeping Adam."
>
> —Pope Benedict XVI

What is most significant for our discussion is that when the book of Exodus tells how the Israelites marked the doorposts with the blood of the lamb, it mentions they used a certain kind of plant to dip in the lamb's blood to do so. Can you guess what kind of plant that was? Hyssop!

> "Take a bunch of hyssop and dip it in the blood which is in the basin and touch the lintel and the two doorposts with the blood which is in the basin" (Exodus 12:21-23).

John's mention of the hyssop *does* have rich significance, associating the death of Jesus with the sacrifice of the Passover lamb. The reference to hyssop in the context of the Passover feast would bring to mind the hyssop dipped in the blood of the lamb at the first Passover in Egypt. That is not the only connection.

John earlier noted that Jesus was condemned to death on "the day of Preparation" before the Passover, which is the day the Passover lambs would have been sacrificed. The further detail of the condemnation taking place at "the sixth hour," which is noon, points to Jesus being rejected around the time when the slaughter for the Passover lambs would have begun (John 19:14).[86]

Furthermore, the clearest connection with the Passover lamb is found in John drawing attention to the fact that Jesus' legs were not broken by the Roman soldiers. John does not mention this point to give orthopedic information for a biopsy report. As we have seen, he mentions Christ's unbroken legs to highlight how Jesus dies like the Passover lambs that were sacrificed—lambs whose bones were not to be broken, according to the Law (see Exodus 12:46).

All these details—the Passover context, the unbroken bones, the hyssop, the day of preparation, and the hour of sacrifice—make the point clear. Jesus is the new Passover Lamb. From a human perspective, Jesus on Good Friday might appear as just one of thousands of Jewish men the Romans had crucified throughout the years. John's Gospel, however, reveals much more. Jesus' death is a sacrifice, a Passover sacrifice. And like the first Passover lambs in Egypt, Jesus brings salvation and life to God's people. Just as the Passover lambs were sacrificed in Egypt to spare the firstborn Israelites that night, so Jesus is sacrificed on Calvary to spare the lot of all humanity.

Those Risen from the Dead

We have seen signs in the heavens (the darkness) and signs on earth (the earthquake, the stones splitting, and a temple veil being torn in two). Now we come to a sign *under* the earth as Matthew reports a most extraordinary event: tombs were

---

[86] Brown, *The Gospel According to John XII-XXI*, 883, 895. See also Keener, *The Gospel of John*, 1130.

opened and "many of the bodies of the saints who had fallen asleep were raised" (Matthew 27:52).

In the Jewish tradition, one of the key signs of "the age to come" was the resurrection of the faithful. In fact, the only reference in the entire Old Testament to tombs being opened comes in the resurrection prophecy of Ezekiel 37. The prophecy tells of the restoration of Israel and the new era when God's exiled people will dwell in the land again.

In the passage, Ezekiel is given a vision of God breathing life into dry bones that fill a valley. The bones come together, skin covers them, and they stand on their feet. The Lord explains to Ezekiel the meaning of the vision: the prophecy of resurrection symbolizes Israel's return to the land after being in exile. This is a fitting image, for in the Bible, the curse of exile was described as a kind of death (see Deuteronomy 30:15-20). In exile, God's people, therefore, were like the dry bones in the valley. But when they return to the land, they will experience a kind of resurrection. "I will open your graves and raise you from your graves, O my people; and I will bring you home to the land of Israel ... I will put my Spirit within you and you shall live, and I will place you in your own land" (Ezekiel 37:12,14).

The tombs being opened at Jesus' death recalls this prophecy of hope. It signals a new day is dawning for Israel. It not only anticipates the final resurrection of all at the end of time, but also reveals God's power being unleashed right now, in the present, breaking in the new age that Ezekiel foretold.[87]

---

[87] Matthew also notes many bodies of the saints were raised, came out of the tombs, and were seen by many after Jesus' resurrection (Matthew 27:52). Such an event exhibits the power of Jesus' resurrection and Matthew mentions it here in his narrative to give another ray of hope amid the darkness of Good Friday. The placement of this event here underscores how Jesus' death is not a moment of defeat but of triumph. His sacrificial death brings victory over death for all. Indeed, the event is a sign of how Jesus' resurrection is the source of life to all who have fallen asleep. He is "the first-born from the dead" (Colossians 1:18) and the "first fruits of those who have fallen asleep" (1 Corinthians 15:20). Though these saints were raised from the dead, St. Ambrose, St. Augustine, and St. Thomas Aquinas argue that they did not experience a resurrection like Jesus did, but that they were only resuscitated, returning to ordinary bodies and would die again. See Brown, *Death of the Messiah,* 2:1132, n. 90.

The Burial of Jesus

The Romans typically would not allow the crucified body to be given a proper burial. The body would be left on the cross for days or would be thrown to the ground where it would be eaten by animals or suffer natural decay. But Jewish law called for the burial of the executed man's body, not allowing it to remain hanging overnight (see Deuteronomy 21:22-23). For the Jews, taking care of dead bodies that were not given any burial provision was an act of charity (see Tobit 1:16-18), and usually those bodies were given a simple, common burial plot.

These Jewish sensitivities are certainly part of what drove a man named Joseph of Arimathea to ask Pilate for Christ's body to bury it. But the kind of burial that he and a man named Nicodemus gave Jesus is extraordinary. The fact that Jesus' body is buried in a new, rock-cut family tomb, wrapped in fine cloth, and given an excessive amount of spices for an initial anointing, shows that Joseph and Nicodemus were motivated by much more than common Jewish piety. Such extravagant care for Jesus' burial expresses a most ardent act of devotion—one fitting for a disciple.

Joseph of Arimathea

Apart from this scene, Joseph of Arimathea is not mentioned elsewhere in Scripture. The few details the Passion narratives offer paint the picture of a faithful disciple. He is from a Judean town, likely about twenty miles northwest of Jerusalem. He seems to have settled in Jerusalem, where he had bought a new tomb for his family (see Matthew 27:60). He must have been an influential leader in Jerusalem to have easy access to Pontius Pilate and ample gravitas in the city to secure from Pilate this request. In fact, Mark mentions how Joseph was "a respected member" of the Sanhedrin (Mark 15:43) and a rich man— echoing the suffering servant prophecy which foretold how the righteous would be buried with the rich: "and they made his grave ... with a rich man in his death, although he had done no violence, and there was no deceit in his mouth" (Isaiah 53:9).

Most significant, the Gospels tell us that Joseph was a disciple of Jesus (see Matthew 27:57), but "secretly for fear of the Jews" (John 19:38). He probably started following Jesus during one of Christ's previous visits to Jerusalem. Luke notes how Joseph was "a good and righteous man" who, similar to the Simeon, "was looking for the kingdom of God" (Luke 23:50). In other words, Joseph of Arimathea was the kind of person well-disposed to read the signs of the times and receive Jesus with faith. Though he was a member of the Sanhedrin, Luke is careful to point out Joseph of Arimathea "had not consented to their purpose and deed" against Jesus (Luke 23:51).

Finally, the story of Joseph of Arimathea at the *end* of Christ's life recalls another famous Joseph from the *start* of Christ's life: Joseph, the husband of Mary. Consider the parallels. Both Josephs are pious Jews, described as "righteous" men (Matthew 1:19, NAB; Luke 23:50, NAB) who act on behalf of a helpless Jesus. Joseph the husband of Mary protects the baby Jesus from Herod's terror, while Joseph of Arimathea ensures Christ's body receives a burial after his crucifixion.

Both stories involve Jewish authorities working with Roman rulers to oppose Jesus. The husband of Mary protects the Christ child after Herod seeks counsel from the chief priests in Jerusalem, while Joseph of Arimathea buries Jesus' body after the chief priests work with the Roman governor Pilate to bring Jesus to his death. Though both Josephs play an important role in the story, neither have a single word quoted in Scripture.[88]

---

[88]   Davies and Allison, *Matthew 19-28*, 656.

Nicodemus

John's Gospel also mentions a man named Nicodemus coming forward to help bury Christ's body. This is the same Nicodemus who earlier in John's Gospel, came to Jesus by night. We know from that previous scene that Nicodemus was a Pharisee who seems to be a well-known "teacher" and served as "a ruler of the Jews" (John 3:1, 10). In other words, like Joseph of Arimathea, Nicodemus was part of the Sanhedrin.

In Nicodemus' first encounter with Jesus, he is confused, does not understand Jesus' teachings, and views Christ primarily as a teacher and wonder worker. Over time, Nicodemus undergoes a change in heart. During one of Jesus' previous visits to Jerusalem, Nicodemus defended Jesus when the chief priests and Pharisees were trying to arrest him (see John 7:50-51). And now, on a day when most of Christ's disciples have abandoned him, Nicodemus is one of the few who shows compassion for Jesus. He comes out to help Joseph of Arimathea bury Christ's body (see John 19:39).

The Women and The Royal Burial

It was "the day of preparation" for the Sabbath. This particular Sabbath was also a feast day—the "great day" of Passover. Therefore, there was even greater pressure to complete the work of burial before the sunset marking the start of the Sabbath rest and to have the body removed in order to maintain the holiness of the feast.

There was no time for a proper burial, which would include cleansing the body, anointing it with oil, and clothing it. Still, though this initial burial was rushed, it was far from ordinary. One hundred Roman pounds of myrrh and aloes were packed around the body to counterbalance the smell of the decaying corpse and slow down corruption until fuller burial procedures could be carried out after the Sabbath. That is what the women at the Cross anticipate as they already start preparing spices and ointments to take with them to the tomb on Easter morning (see Luke 23:56, 24:1).

The details involved in Christ's burial indicate it was meant to be understood as a *royal* one—a burial fit for a king. An extravagant amount of spices would be used in some funerals (see 2 Chronicles 16:14), such as that for Herod the Great, when five hundred servants were needed to carry the spices at his burial.[89] Nicodemus' generosity recalls the extravagance of Mary anointing Jesus' feet with a pound of myrrh in John 12:3.

Nicodemus' gifts to Christ takes generosity to a whole new level. If Mary's one-pound gift of myrrh had been worth 300 denarii (see John12:5), his offering of 100 pounds may have been worth 30,000.[90] Moreover, a new tomb "in which no one had ever been buried" also was an honor fit for a king. And the fact that the tomb is located in a garden adds further royal symbolism, for the kings of Judah (see 2 Kings 21:18, 20), and David himself (see Nehemiah 3:16), were buried in garden tombs.

The Tomb and the Garden

Two important details about the burial tell us about the kind of tomb in which Jesus' body was laid to rest. First, Matthew, Mark and Luke mention that Jesus' burial place was hewn from "*rock*" (Matthew 27:60; Mark 15:46; Luke 23:53). Second, all four Gospels mention a *stone at the entrance of the tomb*. Matthew and Mark note that Joseph of Arimathea rolled a great "stone" against the door of the tomb (Matthew 27:60; Mark 15:46), while Luke and John mention a stone that had been "rolled away from the tomb" on Easter morning (Luke 24:2; John 20:1). The overall description

---

[89]   Josephus, *Antiquities of the Jews*, 17.199.

[90]   Keener, *The Gospel of John*, 2:1163.

indicates the tomb had been formed by quarrying into the side of a rock face and likely had a disc-shaped stone rolled into place in front of the entrance, which was common in that day.

At the request of the chief priests, Pilate assigns soldiers to guard the tomb, and they secured the burial place by sealing the stone. This sealing likely consisted of wax put on the stone at the opening with the imprint of a seal in the wax that would break if the stone was moved, and thus indicate the tomb was opened.[91]

Finally, the mention of the tomb being located in a *garden* offers a ray of hope. While it was common for people to be buried in fields and gardens, John's mention of it at the end of Christ's passion recalls the Garden of Eden. It symbolizes a return to paradise; a reversal of Adam's expulsion from the Garden of Eden and an opening to new life. The very end of Christ's passion story, therefore, brings us back all the way to the beginning, back to the Garden of Eden. Whereas Adam was expelled from the garden which was guarded by the angels (see Genesis 3:24), Jesus will rise from the dead at his garden tomb, which will be marked by the presence of angels on Eastern morning (see Matthew 28:5; Mark 16:5; Luke 24:4). Indeed, John's mention of the tomb in the garden signals hope for all the sons of Adam. On this day of darkness and death, from this garden tomb, there will soon shine the Light of the World who will rise again on the third day.

---

[91] Brown, *Death of the Messiah*, 2:1296.

——————— **REFLECTION QUESTIONS** ———————

- *The Roman centurion is one of the last people we'd expect to come to faith on Good Friday, and yet he does (see Mark 15:39). Who are some people in your life whom you might be tempted to think would never come to embrace the Catholic Faith? What are some specific ways can you pray for them? What might God want you to do to witness the Catholic Faith to them more?*

- *We saw how the water and blood flowing from Christ's side (John 19:34) symbolize baptism and the Eucharist. How do you think these two sacraments keep us close to Jesus, close to "his side," today?*

- *Joseph of Arimathea had been a disciple of Jesus, but "secretly for fear of the Jews" (John 19:38). On Good Friday, however, this man's faith in Jesus dramatically comes out into the public as he boldly asks Pilate for Christ's body and gives Jesus a most honorable burial in his own family tomb. What are some ways you find yourself wanting to live your faith "secretly" for fear of what others might think of you? What can you do practically to live your faith more openly with the people around you?*

- *Imagine being at Calvary and watching all Jesus suffered. Imagine watching him breathe his last breath. At this moment, you suddenly realize he did all this not only to "save the world," but for you, personally. He died for you. How often do you thank the Lord for all he has done for you in his passion and death? What can you do more to express your love and gratitude for him dying for you? Take a moment and thank him right now.*

Part Two:

THE SEVEN LAST WORDS

Jesus is stripped of his garments

Christians have long pondered Christ's "Seven Last Words," which refers to the seven brief sayings Jesus uttered from the Cross before he died. For centuries, these words have been the subject of many sermons, books, devotions, and musical pieces. The fact that there are seven such sayings recorded in Scripture is significant. For in the Bible, seven is the number of perfection—the number of the covenant. It brings to mind the seven days of creation, when God created the world in six days and rested on the seventh. That Jesus gave seven last words before dying points, on one hand, to how Jesus is about to enter into his rest. After completing the work of his ministry, he will enter his sabbath, the sleep of death. On the other hand, it points to how Christ's death will be the beginning of a new creation that is about to be born. His death is not forever. He will rise from the dead and all creation will be renewed.

When a person approaches death, their last words to us often have great significance. They can serve as a window into what is most important to the dying person. This is especially the case with Jesus. As St. Augustine states, "The tree upon which were fixed the members of Him dying was even the chair of the Master teaching."[92]

Think of these seven last words not merely as words spoken to the world in general, but as personal words, spoken to you. Before Jesus died, he was thinking of you and what you would be going through this year, this month, this day. He wants to give you a certain message to encourage you, comfort you, or challenge you.

The Seven Last, Words are:

"Father, Forgive Them; For They Know Not What They Do" (Luke 23:34).

"Today You Will Be with Me in Paradise" (Luke 23:43).

"Behold, Your Son ... Behold, Your Mother" (John 19:26-27).

"My God, My God, Why Have You Forsaken Me?" (Matthew 27:46).

"I Thirst" (John 19:28).

"It Is Finished" (John 19:30).

"Father, Into Your Hands I Commit My Spirit" (Luke 23:46).

The reflections that follow can be used simply to continue our biblical journey through Christ's passion and learn more about Jesus' words from the Cross. Or they can be used as a prayerful devotion, especially during Lent. Since there are seven, you can spread them out over the course of one week, doing one reflection each day. Or you can read them all on one day, perhaps on Good Friday or another day you set aside for extra prayer.

Let us consider the biblical background for each of these words and how Jesus continues to speak to us today through them.

---

[92] As quoted in St. Thomas Aquinas, *Summa Theologica*, III.46.4.

Chapter Sixteen

"FATHER, FORGIVE THEM; FOR THEY KNOW NOT WHAT THEY DO"
(LUKE 23:34)

Rock of Calvary in the Chapel of Adam, Church of the Holy Sepulchre

The Roman soldiers might have expected a cry from Jesus when he was nailed to the Cross. A cry of pain. A cry of despair. A cry of anger. A cry cursing his executioners. Those are the kinds of cries the soldiers would have heard from the cross. But the last thing they would have expected to hear from a man they just crucified is this:

"Father, forgive them; for they know not what they do" (Luke 23:34).

These represent the first words Jesus spoke just after being nailed to the Cross. As surprising as they would have been to the Roman soldiers who drove the nails into his body, these words should not, however, be a shock to us readers of the Gospels.

For this is exactly what Jesus had been talking about from the beginning of his public ministry: Love your enemy. Pray for those who persecute you. Forgive those who trespass against us. Now Jesus gives a powerful concrete example of what he himself taught.

Admittedly, this kind of forgiveness is hard. How can we forgive someone who has hurt us deeply? The Catechism teaches that it may not always be in our power not to feel a wound that has been inflicted upon us. Neither do we always have the ability to forget the hurt. Nevertheless, the Church teaches that there are two things we can do when someone has injured us. We always have the capacity to turn that hurt into *intercession* and turn it into *compassion*. Let's take a closer look at these two aspects over which we do have control and how Jesus models them for us in his prayer for his enemies on Good Friday.

Intercession

First, Jesus *intercedes* for the people who are responsible for his crucifixion. He prays for the Father to forgive them. The word in Greek for forgive is *aphiemi*, which literally means: set aside, let go, or release. The image is a beautiful one, presenting Jesus in Luke as praying that his enemies be *released* or *set free* by God from their sins. "The liberty [*aphesis*] proclaimed by Jesus in Nazareth is here offered to his enemies, preparing also for the disciples' proclamation of 'forgiveness' [*aphesis*] to all the nations."[93]

That is something that we can do, too. When someone has hurt us—whether a family member, friend, coworker, or even someone in our parish—we can always pray for that person. That does not require us having warm feelings for the person. After all, there is a big difference between *liking* and *loving* someone. Liking involves feelings. Webster's dictionary says

---

[93] Pablo Gadenz, *The Gospel of Luke* (Grand Rapids, MI: Baker Academic, 2018), 381, on Luke 4:18. 24:47.

the verb "like" means to feel attraction toward, take pleasure in, or enjoy. The virtue of love, however, goes beyond our emotions and resides in the will. Love is a decision, a choice to act toward the good of the person we love. As the Catechism explains, to love is to will the good of the other, to seek what's best for the other person.[94]

That's something we can do even for our enemies. We might not be able to *like* a certain person in the sense of taking delight in him or enjoying being around him. But we are called to *love* everyone—even those who hurt us. If love resides in the will, we can, therefore, still desire their good and seek what is best for them, no matter what kind of feelings we may have for them. We can pray for them: that God may bless them, that they do God's will, that they experience God's love, and that they grow in faith. We can also offer sacrifices and our Holy Communion for them. These are beautiful acts of love which we can offer for anyone, especially those who hurt us.

In other words, we can turn the hurt into intercession. And sometimes that requires tremendous inner strength to rise above our emotions. We must always resist the temptation to turn our hurt into hate. It is always wrong to wish the one who hurt us harm, to hope for vengeance, or even to act toward his demise. If we notice the slightest trace of that kind of hatred growing in our hearts, one of the best things we can do to eradicate that brewing malice is to pray for that person. In this way, we turn the hurt into intercession, not hate. If you find yourself in a more intense, traumatic situation unable to pray for the person who hurt you, simply ask God to give you the grace to pray for the person. "Lord, please help me to want to pray for this person." That alone is a small act of love that can drive the demons of hatred away.

---

[94] CCC 1766.

Compassion

Second, Jesus turns the injury into *compassion*. Notice how he does not say, "Father, nothing needs to be forgiven. We are all good. This crucifixion … it's no big deal. It's all OK." No. It *is* a big deal. It's definitely *not* OK. What his persecutors did to Jesus that day was the worst sin in the history of the world—the murder of the Son of God. That fact cannot be overlooked. It must be addressed and dealt with.

At the same time, Jesus also does not vehemently respond, "Father, pour out your wrath on these wicked people for what they've done to me!" No. Jesus sees more than the tragic legal fact of their sin. He also sees their hearts and realizes that they do not fully understand their actions—"they know not what do."

Often in life, we hurt each other but not out of spite, intentionally wanting people around us to suffer. Sometimes it is a matter of our lack of thoughtfulness, or impatience, or self-preoccupation that causes friction in our relationships. That does not excuse someone's sins, but it is helpful to recognize that the other person is not deliberately looking for ways to make our lives miserable, thinking, *How can I make my spouse or coworker upset today?* Many times, the people who hurt us do not even know what they are doing.

This is especially true in marriage. How many times do spouses hurt each other, not out of evil intentions, but because they fail to anticipate how their actions will affect their beloved? There are many husbands and wives who love their spouse and do not want to do anything to hurt their beloved, but they still do, simply because they do not understand what they are doing.

Jesus models for couples how to avoid judging our spouse's heart and intention. His example challenges us to avoid assuming our beloved does not care or intentionally wants to hurt us. We must see beyond the surface—the frustrated look, the harsh tone, the absent *thank you*, the persistent nagging, the lack of time and attention, or the self-centeredness. We must not accuse the *heart* of our beloved. When we do that, walls build up in a marriage and potentially years of hurt, dysfunction, and resentment. Remember, it is the devil who is the accuser, and his voice of accusation constantly speaks into the ears of married couples: *He'll never change ... Why doesn't she understand? ... There he goes again ... She just doesn't respect me ... It's his fault. I didn't do anything wrong ... She doesn't care ... He never has time for me.* The devil wants us to accuse our beloved and build those walls around our hearts to divide our marriages.

Jesus calls us to resist that temptation—to rebuke the voice of the evil one—and see beyond the hurt to realize that our beloved may still truly love us and not fully realize what they are doing. Maybe they are having a rough day or not feeling well. Maybe they are hurt by something or stressed out. Maybe they are responding a certain way because of their upbringing or a deep wound from their past. None of this excuses our beloved's unvirtuous words or actions, but it does help us respond with greater patience and compassion. After all, that is what Jesus did for his bride, the people of God, who rejected him that day. Jesus said, "Father, forgive them; for they know not what they do."

──────── **REFLECTION QUESTIONS** ────────

- *Imagine being one of the soldiers who drove the nails into Christ's hands. How would you feel hearing Jesus pray, "Father, forgive them; For they know not what they do"?*

- *On the Cross, Jesus prays for those who do him harm. Think of someone who has hurt you deeply. How easy is it for you to forgive that person? Is it possible to forgive someone even while still feeling the pains or the memories of the hurt you endured? How might turning your hurt into intercession for that person help you love the one who hurt you?*

- *When forgiving his persecutors, Jesus also said, "They know not what they do." How might these words inspire us to have compassion on those who have wounded us?*

Chapter Seventeen

"TODAY YOU WILL BE WITH ME IN PARADISE"
(Luke 23:43)

Crucifixion by Antonello da Messina

If you have ever attended a Good Friday service, you may have heard these words sung during the liturgy: "Jesus, remember me when you come into your kingdom." The whole hymn is just this one line that is repeated over and over again, echoing what the "good thief" said to Jesus on the Cross.

It is fitting that the words are sung in a repeated fashion, for the Gospel of Luke tells us that the good thief himself did not speak these words only once but had been repeating those words to Jesus. He "*was saying*, 'Jesus, remember me when you come in your kingly power'" (Luke 23:42).

Jesus eventually answered his persistent prayer in what has come to be known as the second of the last seven words of Christ from the Cross. To appreciate those sacred words, let us step back and consider the scene as a whole.

Good Thief, Bad Thief

We know the good thief was not always so good. As we have seen, the word for thief (*lestes*) was used to describe violent criminals and revolutionaries. Indeed, crucifixion was not a common punishment for pickpocketing or house robbery. It was a penalty for those who used violence in rising up against Rome. This man, therefore, would have been a part of the very movement Jesus' ministry of peace, humility, and forgiveness would have opposed.

That is not all. This man did not just carry some sin from the past. He was committing grave offenses against God right there on Calvary. For as Matthew's Gospel makes clear, the good thief was someone who mocked Jesus on Good Friday, joining the others at the foot of the Cross who were reviling Jesus (see Matthew 27:44).

Yet, in those hours on the Cross, something changed inside him. Something moved him to have a change of heart. Perhaps it was the witness of Jesus refusing the pain-dulling wine mixed with myrrh and enduring his suffering so patiently. Maybe it was how Jesus forgave his enemies from the Cross. Maybe it was simply the man realizing his life was drawing to a close and his need to reconcile with God.

Whatever the case may be, the man repents of his sins and turns to Jesus before he dies. In the process, he models three key steps of repentance we can apply to our own lives. The next time you have a sin you need to repent of—however big or small—follow these three steps of the good thief on Good Friday.

STEP ONE: Rebuke the Voice of the Enemy

First, he "rebuked" the other thief. The other criminal continued mocking Jesus, saying, "Are you not the Christ? Save yourself and us!" (Luke 23:39). The good thief "rebuked" him (Luke 23:40). That word Luke uses for "rebuked" (*eptimaō*) is an important one. It can refer to reproaching not merely someone with whom one disagrees, but a much fiercer opponent. Think about it. Who is often *rebuked* in the Gospels? The devil. In fact, in Luke's Gospel, the good thief rebuking the other criminal recalls how Jesus rebuked Satan and evil spirits in his public ministry (see Luke 4:35, 39, 41).

That is a significant point. We saw in chapter fourteen how the crucified criminals joined the chief priests and those passing by in attacking Christ's divine sonship. As they said, "If you are the Son of God, come down from the cross," they were echoing the voice of Satan who said to Jesus similar words when tempting him in the desert: "If you are the Son of God …" (see Matthew 4:3, 6, and 27:40, 43). Now, as this one good thief starts to repent of this mocking, it's fitting that he's described as having "rebuked" the other criminal who persisted in reviling Christ. For that other criminal, in attacking Christ's divine sonship, was echoing the voice of Satan and thus deserves to be rebuked like Satan.

This offers an important lesson for us. One first step in repenting is to rebuke the voice of Satan, which does everything it can to prevent us from turning away from sin and turning toward God's mercy. Satan's voice often works in two ways. On one hand, Satan is called the accuser and he likes to indict us, putting self-condemning thoughts in our heads: "You're so horrible. You'll never change. It's too hard; why bother trying? Everyone else is so much better than you. You can't be forgiven." He will discourage us and get us to focus on our sins, to compare ourselves to other Christians who seem to be living the faith so much better, and to think we are failures.

He'll also push us to despair, getting us to think that we can never overcome our weaknesses, sins, and addictions, that we should just throw in the towel and not fight the battle anymore. We must rebuke that voice of Satan, for it keeps us focused on ourselves, stuck in our sins, and prevents us from turning to God's mercy. No matter what we have done, our sins do not have to define us—if we repent and throw ourselves into the arms of the Father's mercy.

Justifying Our Sin

Satan also uses the voice of rationalization, getting us to justify the wrong we are doing: *It's OK … It's not a big deal … I only did it once … The company won't notice … What I do with my boyfriend doesn't matter … I'm not hurting anyone … Everybody else watches that show … I'm not a bad person …* Or it gets us to blame other people for our actions: *She started it … So it's her fault … He's never going to change, so I have to take matters in my own hands … But if my boss didn't treat me this way, I wouldn't need to do this …* These voices of rationalization are trying to silence our conscience, to keep us from admitting our sin and turning back to God. Deep down, we sense that what we are doing might be wrong, but the rationalizing thoughts quickly step in to justify our actions and cover up any sense of remorse we might have, stifling the movements of the Holy Spirit in our hearts. Instead of acknowledging the truth of our actions and turning to God to help us change, we rationalize our actions, never grow, and remain stuck in our sins.

Like the good thief, the first step in turning away from sin is to rebuke the voices of Satan—the voices of self-condemnation and rationalization. The next time you find yourself discouraged about your weaknesses, rebuke that voice of the accuser in your head. Say a quick prayer. Call on Jesus' name. Make the Sign of the Cross. Similarly, the next time you notice yourself feeling badly about something you did, something you said, or something you failed to do—do not let the voice of rationalization keep you from going to confession or saying sorry to your spouse, your friend, your boss, or God. Talk to God about what happened. Ask him what he thinks. Tell God you do not want to be willful and rationalize your sin. Rebuke the voice of rationalization and tell God sorry right away. Tell the person you hurt or let down sorry. Get to the confessional.

STEP TWO: Name Our Sin

One of my children, when he realized he did something wrong when he was younger, would hide in a closet. Sometimes he felt ashamed over what he did and did not want to be seen by others. Other times, he simply did not want to face mom and dad asking him about his behavior and the punishment that likely would follow. In either case, he wanted his actions to remain hidden, in the dark. He was afraid to step out into the light.

When we rebuke the accusing and rationalizing voices, we do not have to hide. We have the confidence to bring our sins out into the open—to admit them, name them, own them. That is why the sacrament of reconciliation is so freeing. We have a space to be totally authentic, vulnerable before the priest, before God, and before our fragile selves to face the honest truth about ourselves. It is only then that we pave the way to experience the Father's love and forgiveness. Only then can we experience his encouragement to get up and try again and his healing grace to help us be better next time.

All this is modeled by the good thief's second move. After rebuking the other criminal, he brings his own sinfulness out into the light. He acknowledges his wrongdoing and admits he is deserving this punishment: "Do you not fear God, since you are under the same condemnation? And we indeed justly; for we are receiving the due reward of our deeds" (Luke 23:41). In his dying moments, the man turns away from the bitter resentment he exhibited when he was mocking Jesus on Calvary. He also does not try to cover up his wrongdoing anymore and justify his actions. He looks it square in the eye and faces the truth of his sin. "We are receiving the due reward of our deeds." Now he can open himself up to the next step: encountering God's mercy.

STEP THREE: Entrust Yourself to Jesus' Mercy

Having admitted his sins, the good thief then does something no one else in the Gospels ever does. He addresses Jesus by his personal name: "*Jesus*, remember me when you come into your kingly power" (Luke 23:42, emphasis added). Others address Jesus by name but always with a reverential title, such as "Jesus, Son of the Most High God" (Mark 5:7; Luke 8:28); "Jesus, Son of David" (Mark 10:47; Luke 18:38); "Jesus, Master" (Luke 17:13); or some qualification, such as "Jesus of Nazareth" (Mark 1:24; Luke 4:34).

The good thief is the only person in the Gospels to address Jesus simply by name. The confidence and intimacy is remarkable, especially given the fact of where this man was spiritually only a few hours before. Having rebuked those voices at the Cross (step one) and admitted his sin (step two), the good thief finds a new confidence. He turns to Christ and addresses him personally, intimately, as a friend—"Jesus"—and he humbly places all his trust in Christ's mercy (step three).

He also recognizes what the chief priests, Pilate, and Herod failed to grasp that day: that the mocked, scourged, and crucified Jesus is the true King the people have been longing for. In fact, he is the first to see how Jesus' crucifixion is not contradictory to his being the messiah-king but is part of his enthronement. So much does he trust in Jesus being Israel's messiah-king, he says, "Jesus, remember me when you come into your kingly power" (Luke 24:42). His words recall biblical prayers of trusting in God's mercy such as Psalm 25:7, which expresses the good thief's situation quite well: "Remember not the sins of my youth, or my transgressions; according to your mercy remember me, for your goodness' sake, O LORD!" He believes the dying Jesus will be vindicated and receive his kingdom, and the good thief wants to be remembered at that moment. As Benedict XVI explains, the good thief

> The good thief is the only person in the Gospels to address Jesus simply by name.

"realized that this powerless man was the true king—the one for whom Israel was waiting. Now he wanted to be at this man's side not only on the Cross, but also in glory."[95]

The good thief makes a bold request, but Jesus gives him even more than he asked for. He responds, "Truly I say to you, today you will be with me in paradise" (Luke 23:43). Whereas the thief asked simply to be remembered, Jesus offers him paradise![96]

In the Jewish tradition, the word "paradise" refers to where the righteous dwell in blessedness after death.[97] In the Septuagint (the early translation of the Greek Old Testament), the Garden of Eden was considered an earthly paradise (see Genesis 2:8, 13:10; Ezekiel 31:8) where Adam originally resided. After the Fall, he was expelled from paradise and it remained closed to the sinful human family up to the time of Christ (Genesis 3:23-24 LXX).

Now, the gates to paradise will be opened again. We have already seen how the Gospels portray Jesus in his passion as a New Adam, taking on the curses of the first Adam. After Jesus dies on

---

[95] Benedict XVI, *Jesus of Nazareth: Holy Week,* 212.

[96] As St. Ambrose commented, "More abundant is the favor shown than the request made." *Exposition on the Gospel of Luke,* 10.121.

[97] 1 Enoch 17-19, 32:3, 60:8, 61:12; 2 Enoch 65:10; Ps. Solomon 14:3; T. Leviticus 18:10-11. See also Isaiah 51:3; Ezekiel 28:13, 31:8 where the word refers to the eschataological paradise or garden. See Bock, *Luke 9:51-24:53,* 1857.

the Cross, he will emerge as the New Adam reopening paradise,[98] and he promises that the good thief will be with him.

In Scripture, Eden (Paradise) imagery describes the future glory of Zion (see Isaiah 51:3) and the book of Revelation uses paradise imagery to depict the perfect and lasting happiness the saints have with God (see Revelation 22:2). By bringing the good thief with him to paradise, Jesus is undoing the effects of Adam's sin which prevented humanity from having access to Eden and the Tree of Life ever since the Fall (see Genesis 3:24).[99] And this criminal will be one of the first recipients of this blessing.

Never Too Late

The story of the good thief reminds us that it is never too late to turn to Christ with our sins. Our past does not have to define us. No matter what we have done, and no matter how long we have been away, Jesus is waiting for us—especially in the sacrament of reconciliation. And like the good thief, we may find more is waiting for us there than we expect. Jesus did not say to the good thief, "It's about time you repented! Did you really have to wait to the last minute to get your act together?" No. Jesus lovingly welcomes the criminal's change of heart and says he will be with him in paradise that very day.

The same Jesus who rose the dead and forgave people's sins throughout his public ministry can forgive this man's sins from the Cross and make him a disciple. Indeed, Jesus offers him not just forgiveness, but intimacy: "You will be with me." Jesus is giving this man the status of a disciple, for being with Jesus is a crucial part of what it means to follow Jesus as a disciple (see Luke 22:28-30; Mark 3:14). And that is what Jesus wants for all of us. He does not just want to pardon our offenses, like a judge. He

---

[98]   Jerome Neyrey, *The Passion According to Luke* (Mahwah, NJ: Paulist Press, 1985), 180-184.

[99]   Brown, *Death of the Messiah,* 2:1011-2.

wants our hearts, like a lover. He longs for us to be intimately close to him. What he offered the good thief, he offers us today and every day if we turn to him—divine intimacy. For he said, *"You will be with me."* As St. Ambrose commented, "Life is to be with Christ; for where Christ is, there is the kingdom."[100] And if we remain faithful to him to the end, we too can be with Jesus forever in paradise.

──────── **REFLECTION QUESTIONS** ────────

- *This chapter discussed how when we sin, we must rebuke the voices of "self-condemnation" and "rationalization." What are the differences between these two voices? Which one do you tend to struggle with more?*

- *How does rebuking the voices of "self-condemnation" and "rationalization" give us a safe space to face the truth of our sins like the "good thief" did at Calvary?*

- *The "good thief" repents and finds an intimacy with Christ no one else in the Gospels up to this point experiences. He addresses Christ personally by name, "Jesus," and he is told he will be with Jesus in paradise on this day. Do you believe you can ever have this kind of closeness with Christ—even with all your sins? How might the closeness this great sinner discovers in Christ encourage you?*

────────────

[100] Ambrose, *Expositio Evang. Secundum Lucam* 10.121 (CC14:379).

Chapter Eighteen

"BEHOLD, YOUR SON ... BEHOLD, YOUR MOTHER"

(John 19:26-27)

Mosaic, Church of the Holy Sepulchre, Jerusalem

In his dying moments, Jesus was thinking of you, wanting to give you one last precious gift that was dear to his own heart—his mother Mary. He said from the Cross, "Behold, your mother."

> But standing by the cross of Jesus were his mother, and his mother's sister, Mary the wife of Clopas, and Mary Magdalene. When Jesus saw his mother, and the disciple whom he loved standing near, he said to his mother, "Woman, behold, your son!" Then, he said to the disciple, "Behold, your mother!" And from that hour the disciple took her to his own home. (John 19:25-27)

On a basic level, these touching final words to Mary and his beloved disciple reveal Jesus' loving care for his mother. Just before he dies, Jesus thinks about how his mother will be cared for after his death, and he entrusts her to his closest disciple.

But there is also something more. It seems unlikely that Christ's words here are only about Jesus' care for Mary's material, human needs. In John's Gospel, Jesus is often raising people's attention above the material and natural to the more spiritual and supernatural. The miraculous wine at Cana, for example, is not just about a beverage for the wedding feast, but points to the symbolic messianic wine foretold by the prophets (see John 2:1-11). Similarly, Jesus speaking about being "born again" is not about returning to the mother's womb but receiving new life from the Father and becoming a child of God (see John 3:1-8). The "bread of life" Jesus speaks of is not about loaves for dinner, but the gift of his Body in the Eucharist (see John 6:35-65). Especially at the Cross, where every scene is filled with much theological symbolism and prophecy fulfillment, there must be something much more profound in Jesus' words "Behold, your mother" than merely the human, this-worldly concern of making sure someone looks after his mom after he dies.

One key to unlocking the deeper meaning of this passage with Jesus and Mary is to understand the symbolic role the third major character—the beloved disciple—plays in this account from John's Gospel.

The Beloved Disciple

Traditionally, the beloved disciple has been identified as the apostle John. But the Fourth Gospel often uses individual characters to symbolize larger groups. Nicodemus, for example, is described as "a man of the Pharisees" and a "ruler of the Jews" who comes to Jesus by night and does not understand Jesus' teachings (John 3:1). Nicodemus is an individual who represents the many Pharisees and other Jewish leaders who do not understand Christ and are left, like him, in the dark. Similarly, the Samaritan woman at the well who has difficulty understanding Jesus' words, but later comes to faith, represents the many Samaritans who have fallen away from Judaism, but will come to believe in Christ (see John 4:41-42).

A closer look at the beloved disciple suggests that this figure also represents more than an individual follower of Christ. He represents the *ideal* disciple. The beloved disciple is the one who is close to Jesus, leaning on his master's breast at the Last Supper (see John 13:25). He is the one apostle who remains with Jesus even in the face of Christ's suffering and persecution. While the other apostles fled from Christ, the beloved disciple is the only one of the Twelve who followed Jesus all the way to the Cross (see John 19:26). The beloved disciple also is the first to arrive at the tomb on Easter Sunday, the first to believe in Christ's resurrection (see John 20:8), and the first to bear witness to the risen Christ's Lordship (see John 21:7, 21:24).

Therefore, while the beloved disciple is traditionally identified as the individual apostle John, he also serves as a symbolic representative of *all* faithful disciples. The beloved disciple stands for all those who intimately follow Christ, who are willing to go the Cross, believe in Jesus and bear witness to him as Lord. In other words, this individual disciple represents all beloved disciples of Jesus.

Mother of All Christians

This has important implications for understanding Mary's role in our lives today. In Jesus' last act before he dies, he entrusts this beloved disciple into a maternal relationship with Mary. Since the beloved disciple represents all faithful disciples, this passage can offer important biblical support for the doctrine of Mary's spiritual motherhood over all Christians (see CCC 968-970). At Calvary, Mary becomes the mother of the beloved disciple, but in John's Gospel, this beloved disciple represents all faithful disciples. Thus, one can conclude that Mary is the mother of all the faithful followers of Jesus who are represented by the beloved disciple.[101]

When we read this passage today, we can imagine Jesus is looking at us personally from the Cross and saying, "Behold, your mother!" How would you respond? As our spiritual mother, Mary loves us with a mother's love. She is always looking out for our needs and constantly interceding for us. Will you treasure and welcome this gift of Mary that Jesus gave us on Good Friday?

REFLECTION QUESTIONS

- *Who is the beloved disciple? And why should we see ourselves in this character in John's Gospel?*

- *Put yourself in the shoes of the beloved disciple at Calvary. Imagine Jesus saying to you, "Behold, your mother." How would you feel at that moment as you are being entrusted with Mary?*

- *In one of his last acts from the Cross, Jesus gives Mary to the beloved disciple—and hence to all of us—as a spiritual mother who constantly prays for us with a maternal heart. What can you do to grow in your relationship with Mary and welcome this great gift Jesus gave us from Calvary?*

---

[101] For more on how Jesus' words to Mary and the beloved disciple shed light on Mary's spiritual motherhood over all Christians, see Edward Sri, *Rediscovering Mary in the New Testament* (San Francisco: Ignatius, 2018), 181-192.

Chapter Nineteen

"MY GOD, MY GOD, WHY HAVE YOU FORSAKEN ME?"
(Matthew 27:46)

Christ Crucified by Diego Velázquez

Each Holy Week in the Liturgy we sing the words Jesus cried from the Cross, "My God, my God, why have you abandoned me?" (see Matthew 27:46). Few words capture the depth of Jesus' suffering on Calvary more than these.

But what do these words actually mean?

We are going to see that Jesus is not primarily making a statement about his forsakenness. He is quoting a line from Psalm 22—a psalm with which many in the first century Jewish world would have been familiar and one we have seen alluded to multiple times in the Passion narratives. The background of this psalm makes clear that Jesus' cry from the Cross was far from a cry of despair. It was more a cry of hope in the midst of darkness—and one that can be a great encouragement to us also in the trials we face today.

Why Have You Forsaken Me?

Ancient Jewish rabbis often quoted a line from Scripture to bring to mind the whole context of a particular passage. We might do something similar in our own cultural setting today. Imagine, for example, if we were watching the Olympics, and you asked me, "Which country won the gold medal?" What would you think if I replied, singing, "Oh, say can you see ... by the dawn's early light ... "? My response clearly is not about me inquiring about the quality of your eyesight in the early morning hours. You would immediately catch the allusion to the *Star-Spangled Banner*. You would understand I was singing the USA's national anthem to indicate that the USA won the gold medal.

> Was Jesus really abandoned by His Father on Good Friday?

Similarly, if you asked me which bands I listened to when I was in college, and I responded, "*It's a beautiful day ... But I still haven't found what I'm looking for ...* And I'll have to ponder his question *with or without you.*" To those who do not know these pop cultural references, it sounds like I am talking gibberish. But those familiar with the band U2 would quickly recognize that I am quoting lines from some of their famous songs. I am clearly signaling that it was their music I often had listened to when growing up.

Similarly, when Jesus says, "My God, My God, why have you forsaken me?," he is not focusing our attention merely on those particular words. He is quoting the first line of a famous song in ancient Judaism, a sacred song: Psalm 22. And he wants us to be thinking of the message of the song as a whole, not just the particular line. So, let us step back and consider the background of Psalm 22 as the key to unlocking Jesus' mysterious cry from the Cross.

In You Our Fathers Trusted

Psalm 22 features a righteous man being persecuted by his enemies. He experiences great anguish, so much so that it feels as if he is abandoned by God. The man cries out:

> My God, my God, why have you forsaken me?
> Why are you so far from helping me,
> from the words of my groaning?
> O my God, I cry by day, but you do not answer;
> and by night, but find no rest. (Psalm 22:1-2)

If the Psalm ended there, it would give the impression of a man in despair. But the man goes on to do what we should all do whenever we face times of trouble: remember our story. We must go to the saints who have gone before us and see how God helped them in their moments of trial. That is what the persecuted man does in the next three verses of Psalm 22. He remembers God's faithfulness—how God helped his ancestors through their tribulations. It gives him confidence that the God who rescued his forefathers will come and rescue him.

> Yet you are holy,
> enthroned on the praises of Israel.
> In you our fathers trusted;
> they trusted, and you did deliver them.
> To you they cried, and were saved;
> In you they trusted, and were not disappointed.
> (Psalm 22:3-5)

These are not the words of a man in despair. These are the words of someone who feels as if God has abandoned him. Nevertheless, remembering God's faithfulness in the past gives him confidence in his present ordeal to trust that the Lord will rescue him.

The psalm moves back and forth like this between the anguish he experiences and the hope he has in the Lord to help him. On one level, he describes many sufferings that foreshadow what Jesus experiences on Good Friday. Consider just five of the most obvious parallels. We have touched on these before but feel the weight of how they all come together in this one Psalm to prefigure Christ on the Cross:

First, the man says, "All who seek me mock at me" (Psalm 22:7). This foreshadows how Jesus is mocked several times by the people at Calvary.

Second, the man says, "They make mouths at me, they wag their heads" (Psalm 22:7). This prefigures how those passing by Calvary deride him, "wagging their heads" (Matthew 27:39).

Third, those persecuting the righteous man say, "He committed his cause to the LORD; let him deliver him, let him rescue him, for he delights in him!" (Psalm 22:8). This anticipates what the chief priests say on Calvary: "Let him come down from the cross, and we will believe in him. He trusts in God; let God deliver him now, if he desires him" (Matthew 27:42-43).

Fourth, the man in Psalm 22 notes how his enemies "have pierced my hands and feet" (Psalm 22:16)—pointing to how Jesus' hands and feet will be nailed to the Cross.

Fifth, the psalmist says his enemies "divide my garments among them, and for my clothing they cast lots" (Psalm 22:18)—which, of course, foreshadows how Jesus' garments are divided by the soldiers who cast lots for them.

The many parallels are striking. The persecuted man in Psalm 22 clearly stands as a prophetic foreshadowing of Jesus Christ's sufferings on Calvary. No wonder Jesus had *this* particular psalm on his mind as he was approaching his death on Good Friday!

A Victory Cry

The psalm, however, does not end with suffering and death. The righteous man goes on to praise God for his faithfulness throughout the ages, for helping the afflicted and rescuing him from the mouth of the lion. He even sees that his own suffering is somehow caught up in God's larger plan of salvation to bring all peoples to worship the Lord. The Psalm reaches its climax in verse 27:

> All the ends of the earth shall remember and turn to the LORD:
> and all the families of the nations shall worship before him.
> For dominion belongs to the LORD,
> and he rules over the nations. (Psalm 22:27-28)

With this background in mind, we can see that Jesus' cry from the Cross is far from a cry of despair. It is a cry of great hope in the midst of great darkness. While some Christians interpret these words as Jesus taking on the wrath of God and being utterly rejected and forsaken by his Father, the Catholic Church emphasizes that Jesus did not experience reprobation as if he himself sinned. Instead, we must keep two points in mind: love drove Jesus to unite himself with our sinful humanity so much that he could say in our name, "My God, my God, why have you forsaken me?" (see CCC 603). At the same time, Jesus remains perfectly united with the Father in the midst of this awful darkness. By quoting Psalm 22—a psalm of suffering and hope, darkness and light—Jesus expresses both these points.

This gives us much encouragement when we face trials and darkness of our own. In times when we might wonder where God is amid our afflictions—when we feel as if God has abandoned us—we should do what Jesus did: turn to Psalm 22. In this psalm, we find three crucial things the persecuted man did when facing his sufferings: he named his pain, turned his pain to the Lord, and remembered God's faithfulness.

1. Name the Pain

First, the suffering man in the psalm poured out his heart to God in his agony. He did not ignore his pain or try to run from it. Many people today, however, are too afraid to face the deep fears, sufferings, and wounds in their lives. The loss of a job. The loss of a loved one. A friend who lets you down. A dysfunctional family. Abandonment. Hurts from the past. Many people are too afraid to talk to God about their suffering, so they keep themselves very busy, distracted, and constantly entertained so they do not ever have to think about it. They live each day desperately trying to convince the people around them, and even themselves, that "all is good."

But deep inside, things are *not* "all good." When God draws close to us, he wants to help us in our afflictions and heal us, just like he did the man in Psalm 22. Reopening those wounds can hurt a bit. Jesus is, after all, the divine surgeon. The man in the psalm did the courageous thing: he dared to face the truth about what was really going on in his life. In his prayer, he expressed to God his rejection, suffering, fears, and doubts, holding absolutely nothing back. In sum, *he named his pain.* The man did not speak in vague generalities, but put into words the specifics of his affliction, mentioning the rejection, the mocking, the wagging of heads, the evil doers surrounding him, and the pierced hands and feet.

Sometimes we face such turmoil in life that we have never dared to process it all. We do not even realize how much we are suffering inside. As difficult as it may be, prayerfully naming our pains in the holy presence of God, a spiritual director, or even a counselor, might be what some of us need to come to terms with the truth of where we are really at and what we have been through. Facing that truth—in God's time and in God's way—is a crucial first step if we want the divine physician to act deeply in our lives and heal us.

2. Turn to the Lord

Second, the suffering man cried out to God for help. He did not just stare at his pain in bitterness. Neither was he a self-pitying melancholic like an Eyore in Winnie the Pooh, saying,

"It's so hard being me." Rather, he confidently turned to the Lord with his suffering. "Be not far from me, for trouble is near and there is none to help" (Psalm 22:11).

These words remind us that there are times when we face trials that have no human solution. As the man in Psalm 22 says, "There is none to help." No amount of money, planning, counseling, or networking can solve it all. No friend, spiritual director, or person of influence can be our savior. There are no human supports to get us through. The only thing we can do is to turn to the Lord like the psalmist did, clinging to God in pure faith, trusting that he will help us through this ordeal. "Be not far from me, for trouble is near and there is none to help" (Psalm 22:11).

Here, I think of St. Thérèse of Lisieux who, when dying from tuberculosis, experienced an even greater affliction: a dark night of faith. In her trials, this saint was tempted by many doubts, even being tempted to distrust there really was a heaven and a God waiting for her on the other side of death. In that period, all she could do was cling to pure faith and recite what she knew from her childhood to be true. She wrote, "While I do not have the joy of faith, I am trying to carry out its works at least. I believe I have made more acts of faith in this past year than all through my whole life."[105] She also forced herself to sing the prayers that express the faith: "I sing simply what I WANT TO BELIEVE."[106] She felt as if she were abandoned by God, but turned to the Lord as the psalmist did, persevering in making heroic acts of faith which helped her through.

I also think of Mary at the Cross. At the Annunciation, Mary was given the most extraordinary revelation from the angel Gabriel that her son would be the great Messiah whose kingdom would last forever (see Luke 1:31-33). But on Good Friday, as St. John

---

[105] St. Thérèse of Lisieux, *Story of a Soul* (Washington: ICS Publications, 1976), 213.
[106] Ibid., 214.

Paul II pointed out, Mary's world is turned completely upside down as she witnesses what, to mere human eyes, seems to be "the complete negation of these words"—the complete opposite of all Gabriel told her.[107] Humiliated, scourged, and nailed to a cross by the Romans, the last thing Jesus looks like from a human perspective is a triumphant messiah-king who is the fulfillment of God's plan of salvation for Israel. For Mary, at this moment, there is absolutely no human crutch that can support her. The only thing she can cling to is raw faith—faith that Jesus is the holy Son of God as Gabriel told her; faith that she truly is "the mother of the Lord" as Elizabeth proclaimed; faith that this trial of the "sword" is somehow a part of God's plan as Simeon prophesied in the Temple long ago. According to St. John Paul II, Mary's faith also would include her Son's own prophecy that he "must go to Jerusalem and suffer many things from the elders and chief priests and scribes, and be killed, and on the third day be raised" (Matthew 16:21). Even in this painful obscurity, Mary had a hope that "contained a light stronger than the darkness that reigns in many hearts."[108] And like the suffering man in Psalm 22, she turned to the Lord with the strength of that hope.

3. Remember God's Faithfulness

Third, the suffering man in Psalm 22 remembered God's faithfulness—how his life story is caught up in a much larger story of God's people throughout the ages. He remembered how many other faithful people of God faced ordeals and sufferings, yet they trusted the Lord, and God heard their cries.

It is important to keep before our minds the heroes in salvation history and the lives of the saints who faced many trials, persecutions, and sufferings that are often much more severe than anything we face. Remembering the stories of their

---

[107] St. John Paul II, *Redemptoris Mater,* 18.

[108] St. John Paul II, General Audience, April 2, 1997, in *Theotokos* (Boston: Pauline, 2000), 184.

faithfulness to God and God's faithfulness to them can comfort us. It is reassuring to look to their examples knowing that they persevered and when they cried out to the Lord in their affliction, he rescued them. Their witness reminds us that God is real. The same God who comforted and rescued St. Thérèse in her dark night of faith, Mary at the foot of the Cross, and the persecuted man in Psalm 22 will hear our prayers in our time of distress and rescue us as well. Intentionally making it a priority to fill our minds regularly with those stories from Scripture and the saints will be a much greater resource to us in our trials than most of the images from movies, social media, and Hollywood. The latest joke from your favorite show is not likely to help you when you find yourself facing your own cross. But the words of God in Scripture and the examples of the saints most certainly will. What do you fill your mind with more?

———— REFLECTION QUESTIONS ————

- *Describe a time when you wondered where God was or felt as if you were abandoned by him. How might have Psalm 22 as a whole—the psalm Jesus on the Cross quotes—been an encouragement to you?*

- *The righteous man in Psalm 22 faces intense suffering but remembers God's faithfulness to his ancestors in rescuing them from their afflictions. How does remembering God's work in the saints and the heroes of the Bible help us in our trials?*

- *Do you fill your mind more with the wisdom of the saints or the trivial from Hollywood, social media, sports, and shows? What will be of greater help to us to navigate the trials in life? What practically can we do to fill our minds a bit more with the wisdom of the saints and Scripture?*

Chapter Twenty

"I THIRST"
(John 19:28)

Re-creation of Calvary

When arriving at Calvary, Jesus rejected the first offer of wine that the soldiers offered him to deaden the pain. We saw how he wanted to remain conscious to the end.

Now, however, as he approaches his final moments, he asks for a drink, saying, "I thirst." John's Gospel says he is given *oxos*, which is the Greek word for "*posca*," the red vinegary wine Roman soldiers, travelers, and peasants would drink. The scene brings to mind what the suffering righteous man in Psalm 69 says, "For my thirst they gave me vinegar to drink" (Psalm 69:21).

It also brings to fulfillment yet another aspect of the "passion psalm" we have encountered multiple times at Calvary: Psalm 22. The persecuted man in this Psalm who is mocked, pierced in his hands and feet, has his garments divided by his enemies who cast lots for his raiment—this man who feels as if he is abandoned by God—also depicts himself as *dying of thirst.*

> My strength is dried up like a potsherd,
> and my tongue cleaves to my jaws;
> You lay me in the dust of death. (Psalm 22:15)

In his dying moments, Jesus cries out in agonizing thirst recalling once again the persecuted man in Psalm 22.[102] But what does Jesus' thirst on the Cross have to do with our lives today?

The Meaning of Jesus' Thirst

Throughout the ages, men and women have expressed the human person's thirst for God. We see this in Psalm 42: "As a deer longs for flowing streams, so longs my soul for you, O God. My soul thirsts for God, for the living God" (Psalm 42:1-2). We see this also in the Catechism, which teaches that the human person has "longings for the infinite" which only God can fulfill (CCC 33). St. Augustine put it best in his prayer to God in the opening of his *Confessions*: "Our heart is restless until it rests in you."

The tradition often has emphasized our thirst for God. One modern saint, St. Teresa of Calcutta (Mother Teresa), did something remarkably different: she focused on *God's* thirst for *us*. The way she expressed it was revolutionary. In my youth, I had heard that Jesus' words from the Cross, "I thirst," expressed his thirst for souls. I understood this more in a general, abstract way in that Jesus wanted souls "out there" in the world to be saved. Mother Teresa, however, saw Jesus' "I thirst" as a very personal statement spoken to each individual today, at every moment. She said Jesus is constantly awaiting our response to his thirst.

> At this most difficult time He proclaimed, 'I thirst.' And people thought He was thirsty in an ordinary way and they gave Him vinegar straight away; but it was not for that thirst; it was for

---

[102] "While thirst is not mentioned in the verse, clearly the sufferer suffers from it to the point of death." Brown, *Death of the Messiah*, 2:1073.

our love, our affection, that intimate attachment to him, and that sharing of His passion. He used, 'I thirst,' instead of 'Give Me your love'... 'I thirst.' Let us hear Him saying it to me and saying it to you.[103]

Jesus' Thirst for You

Mother Teresa made Jesus' statement "I thirst" so personal that she told her sisters to imagine Jesus saying those words directly to them. She even encouraged them to put their own name before "I thirst" and hear Jesus saying, for example, "Sister Mary Vincent, I thirst." We can do the same. We can put ourselves in the silent presence of God, in a quiet place at home or in front of the Blessed Sacrament, and prayerfully imagine Jesus gently calling our name and speaking his parting words from the Cross personally to each of us: "Edward, I thirst."

> Just put yourself in front of the tabernacle. Don't let anything disturb you. Hear your own name and "I Thirst." I thirst for purity, I thirst for poverty, I thirst for obedience, I thirst for that wholehearted love, I thirst for that total surrender. Are we living a deeply contemplative life? He thirsts for that total surrender.[104]

Jesus' "I thirst" from the Cross recalls another moment when Jesus expressed thirst—when he met the woman at the well. He said to her, "Give me a drink" (John 4:7). We are like the Samaritan woman and it is as if Jesus is standing before us today, expressing his thirst and saying, "Give me a drink." Indeed, Jesus is thirsty for something much more than water. He thirsts for us. He thirsts for our love, our attention, our hearts. And one of the key ways we encounter Christ's thirst is in prayer. As the Catechism explains, "It is he who first seeks us and asks us for a drink. Jesus thirsts; his asking arises from the depths of God's desire for us. Whether we realize it or not, prayer is the encounter of God's thirst with ours. God thirsts that we may thirst for him" (CCC 2560).

---

[103] St. Teresa of Calcutta (Mother Teresa), as quoted in Joseph Langford, *Mother Teresa's Secret Fire* (Huntington, IN: OSV, 2008), 281-282.

[104] Mother Teresa, *Where There Is Love, There Is God* (New York: Doubleday, 2012), 52.

——————— REFLECTION QUESTIONS ———————

- *How might the idea of Jesus thirsting for you, personally, change the way you think about your relationship with him?*

- *Imagine being at Calvary and Jesus from the Cross is looking at just you. He gazes into your eyes and addresses you personally, saying your name and then saying, "I thirst." How would you feel? What do you think he wants from you?*

- *The* Catechism *teaches that prayer "is the encounter of God's thirst with ours. God thirsts that we may thirst for him" (CCC 2560). In what ways might this understanding change the way you view prayer?*

Chapter Twenty-One

"IT IS FINISHED"
(John 19:30)

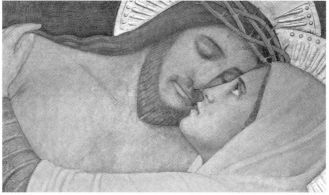

Christ is taken from the Cross

Jesus' words "It is finished" are not a concession speech. This is not a "game over" moment as if time has run out and the other team has more points. Nor is it like the postscript that appears at the end of old movies—"The End"—announcing there is no more to the film. Neither is it about Jesus simply running out of gas, unable to breathe any more, as if he is saying, "I am finished."

Rather, Jesus' words announce a great accomplishment. When he says, "It is finished," he is not announcing something that has merely reached its end, but the completion of something that has reached its intended destination or outcome. He is referring to something that is part of a larger plan and a great work that is now achieved.

What has been brought to completion? The Father's plan from the beginning of time. Jesus himself twice earlier in John's Gospel says that he came to finish the Father's work entrusted to him. And the word he uses at the Cross for "It is finished" (*tetelestai*) is used in those two other passages. "My food is to do the will of him

> Jesus brings to completion what he initiated at the Last Supper.

who sent me, and to accomplish (*telioso*) his work" (John 4:34). Similarly, in Jesus' prayer to the Father at the Last Supper, he states how his ministry finished the work the Father gave him to do: "I glorified you on earth, having accomplished (*teleiōsas*) the work which you gave me to do" (John 17:4). So, on the most fundamental level, by saying, "It is finished," Jesus is announcing that in offering up his life on the Cross, he has accomplished his Father's plan. The Father's plan of salvation from the beginning of time has now been consummated in Jesus' death on Calvary.

The Hour

Other sub-themes in the Gospels are also brought to completion at this moment. The hour of Jesus' glorification, for example, has been accomplished.

Jesus first spoke of his "hour" to his mother at Cana: "My hour has not yet come" (John 2:4). He mysteriously mentions his "hour" several times throughout his public ministry as not being fully here yet, but it finally arrives after Jesus enters Jerusalem riding on a donkey a few days before he dies. Jesus announces, "The hour has come for the Son of man to be glorified" (John 12:23), and he describes his hour of glory as his death, when he will be lifted up from the earth (on the Cross). At that moment of his hour, he says he will do two things: draw all men to himself and defeat the ruler of this world—the devil—who will be cast down (see John 12:31-32).

When Jesus says, "It is finished" just before he dies, this hour of his glory is now complete. The devil is defeated, and Jesus will gather all humanity to himself as he brings salvation to the world just as he foretold.

The Eucharistic Sacrifice

Jesus also brings to completion what he initiated at the Last Supper—the sacrificial offering of his body and blood. Let us go back to that first Eucharist at the Last Supper, which took place in the context of the great Jewish feast called Passover. Consider the meaning of Jesus' words there: "This is my body which is given for you" (Luke 22:19). "This is my blood of the covenant, which is poured out for many for the forgiveness of sins" (Matthew 26:28). We are so familiar with these words because we hear them in the Mass. But if you were one of the apostles present at the Last Supper, one thing that might strike you is that his words about his body being given up and his blood being poured out is sacrificial language—language describing the sacrifices in the Temple and elsewhere in ancient Israel. And what is most astonishing is that Jesus uses this *sacrificial* language in reference to himself! We can see this in many ways.[109]

First, the Passover itself was a sacrifice (see Exodus 12:27). For Jesus to speak about body and blood in the context of Passover would bring to mind the Passover lamb, the blood of which was separated from the body in the ceremonial sacrifice.

Second, when Jesus says his body "will be *given up for you*," the term used in Luke's Gospel for "given up" (*didomai* in Greek) is significant, for it is employed elsewhere in the New Testament in association with sacrifice (see Luke 2:24; Mark 10:45; John 6:51; Galatians 1:4).

---

[109] For more on the biblical background to Jesus' institution of the Eucharist, its sacrificial nature, and how it relates to the Cross and to the Mass, see Edward Sri, *A Biblical Walk Through the Mass* (West Chester, PA: Ascension, 2011), 7-16.

Third, when Jesus speaks of his blood "which will be poured out ... for the forgiveness of sins" (Matthew 26:28), he alludes to the atoning sacrifices in the Temple, which involved blood being poured out over the altar for the purpose of bringing forgiveness (see Leviticus 4:7, 4:18, 4:25, 4:30, 4:34).

Fourth, and perhaps most significantly, Jesus speaks of "the blood of the new and eternal covenant." These words echo what Moses said in the sacrificial ceremony at Mount Sinai that sealed God's covenant union with Israel as his chosen people (see Exodus 24:1-17). In the midst of that sacrificial rite, Moses took the blood of the animals and announced, "Behold the blood of the covenant" (Exodus 24:8). Now, at the Last Supper, Jesus refers to *his* blood as "the blood of the covenant." For the apostles present there, these words could not help but recall what Moses said about the sacrificial blood at Sinai and point to some kind of new sacrifice for a new covenant.

With all these sacrificial themes—the Passover ritual, a body being given up, blood being poured out for forgiveness of sins, and the blood of the covenant—Jesus clearly has some type of sacrifice in mind here. Yet, instead of speaking about the Passover lamb being sacrificed (which is what one might expect in the context of a Passover meal), he talks about his *own* body and blood being offered up and poured out in sacrifice. *His* blood is now the sacrificial blood of the covenant. Jesus thus identifies *himself* with the sacrificial lamb normally offered for Passover. He will be the one whose body will be offered up and whose blood will be poured out in sacrifice on Calvary. The Passover lamb was sacrificed in Egypt to spare the firstborn of the Hebrews, but Jesus, as the new Passover Lamb, offers up his very self as a sacrifice to redeem all humanity, liberating them from sin and death.

Therefore, what Jesus did at the Last Supper mysteriously anticipates his sacrifice on the Cross. There in the upper room,

Jesus willingly offered his body and blood—his whole earthly life—as a sacrifice for the forgiveness of sin. All that was left for him to do was to carry out that offering in a bloody manner on Good Friday. That perfect internal sacrifice of Holy Thursday night was made complete in his crucified body on Good Friday. Therefore, when Jesus says, "It is finished," he is also signaling the completion of the sacrifice he offered in the Eucharistic words he spoke at the Last Supper.

Bringing Your Love to the Finish Line

Do you have areas in your life where you need to grow in sacrificial love? While we can grow in Christ-like love through much study, effort, and prayer, the Mass is the number one place we should go for this, because in the sacred Liturgy, we encounter sacrificial love himself. Jesus' sacrifice on Calvary is made present at every Mass, so we can enter into the dynamic of the Son's perfect offering of love to the Father and be changed by it.

On Good Friday, Jesus said, "It is finished" when he completed his Father's plan of love to save the world. But God next wants to complete that plan in the heart of every believer. So, if you want God's love to transform you—if you want the Father's work to be completed in you and if you long for him one day to say to you, "It is finished"—frequent the Mass. May it lead you on your pilgrimage to becoming a saint. Indeed, may each Eucharist transform your heart with the perfect, sacrificial love of Jesus Christ.

REFLECTION QUESTIONS

- *In what ways is Jesus' saying "It is finished" not an end but a completion of something?*

- *We saw how Christ wants to complete his work of salvation in the life of every individual believer. One of the main ways he does this is through the Mass, where Christ's sacrifice on Calvary is made present to us. How does this understanding change the way you view the Mass? How is the Mass not simply an "obligation"—something we "have to do" each week—but the most profound place we can go to encounter Christ's total, perfect, sacrificial love and be transformed by it?*

- *Throughout this book, we have explored many ways the Old Testament prefigures events in Christ's passion. Which Old Testament connection to Christ do you find most impressive or exciting?*

Chapter Twenty-Two

"FATHER, INTO YOUR HANDS I COMMIT MY SPIRIT"
(Luke 23:46)

Re-creation of the relics of the Crucifixion

When many people looked at the Cross on Good Friday, they saw merely a man scourged, mocked, and killed in a most humiliating and torturous form of execution. Jesus' last words from the Cross underscore how Jesus is not a passive victim. Even to the very end, he remains in charge of his fate. He is not a man who is defeated and simply unable to breathe anymore. Rather, Jesus actively hands over his spirit to the Father, for, as we will see, he has great confidence that the Father will rescue him.

The Loud Cry

Luke tells us Jesus cried out with "a loud voice" (*phonē megalē*)—an expression that is used in varied ways in the New Testament. Sometimes it refers to praising God with a loud voice (see Luke 1:42, 19:37; Revelation 5:12). Other times it is used to describe demons crying out in a loud voice when they are about to be expelled (see Mark 1:26, 5:7; Acts 8:7). But sometimes, it is used in contexts expressing hope in the face of death. Jesus, for example, cried out with a loud voice to call forth the deceased Lazarus from the tomb and bring him back to life (see John 11:43)—an event that foreshadows how all the faithful departed will hear Christ's *voice* and come forth from their tombs in the resurrection of the dead (see John 5:28). Similarly, the great *voice* of the archangel will announce the coming of the Lord to raise all who are dead in Christ (see 1 Thessalonians 4:16). So, when Jesus cries out in a *loud voice*, this does not necessarily mean it is merely a cry of agony, for it could be a cry associated with hope in the face of death.[110]

That this is the case is made clear when we see Jesus quoting the hope-filled Psalm 31 as he confidently commits his spirit to his Father's hands, full of trust that the Father will rescue him.

The psalm itself is the prayer of a righteous man suffering at the hands of his enemies. The man's situation clearly foreshadows what Christ endures on Good Friday. His enemies scheme together against him and plot to take his life (see Psalm 31:13). He is the scorn of his adversaries, and his strength fails him while his bones are wasting away (see Psalm 31:10-11).

Yet, despite these ordeals, the man in Psalm 31 trusts the Lord will come to his assistance.

---

[110] See also Acts 16:28; Revelation 14:28 for other scenes involving a loud cry giving hope for life in the face of death.

> In you, O LORD, do I seek refuge;
> let me never be put to shame;
> in your righteousness deliver me!
> Incline your ear to me,
> rescue me speedily!
> Be a rock of refuge for me, a strong fortress to save me!
> Yes, you are my rock and my fortress;
> for your name's sake lead me and guide me,
> take me out of the net which is hidden for me,
> for you are my refuge.
> Into your hand I commit my spirit;
> you have redeemed me, O LORD, faithful God.
> (Psalm 31:1-5)

Clearly, this is a man who has confidence in the Lord. He trustingly places his life in God's hands and firmly believes he will be protected. The man goes on to conclude by praising the Lord for rescuing him and encourages others to remain courageous in the face of all trials, for the Lord is always faithful.

> Blessed be the LORD
> for he has wondrously shown me his merciful love ...
> You heard my supplications,
> when I cried to you for help.
> Love the LORD, all you his saints!
> The LORD preserves the faithful ...
> Be strong, and let your heart take courage,
> all you who wait for the LORD.
> (Psalm 31:21-24)

The Psalm is obviously a prayer of great hope in the midst of affliction and a fitting final prayer of Jesus as he breathes his last breath. Like the psalmist, Jesus commends his life into God's hands, trusting that his Father will rescue him from death. Indeed, Luke's Gospel tells how Jesus had expressed such trust previously when he spoke about his death and resurrection during his journey to Jerusalem (see Luke 9:22; 18:33) and alluded to it during his trial before the Sanhedrin (see Luke 22:69). Now, in his moment of death, he turns to Psalm 31 as his final prayer and says, "Father, into your hands I commit my spirit."

The Prayer Itself

The prayer itself has two parts: a personal address and a statement of trust.

In his last words, Jesus addresses God personally as "Father"—something he has done before (Luke 10:21, 11:2). In fact, Luke's account of Christ's passion begins on the Mount of Olives with Jesus praying to God as Father. "Father, if you are willing, remove this chalice from me; nevertheless not my will, but yours, be done" (Luke 22:43). How fitting it is that his Passion narrative ends with the similar theme: Jesus is on another mountain—the mount of Jerusalem—and he is intimately addressing his Father again, just as he has finished drinking the cup of suffering he first mentioned in Gethsemane.

His words about committing his spirit to God show him actively handing his life over to the Father. It reminds us of how Jesus said he is the Good Shepherd who *voluntarily* lays down his life for his sheep. "No one takes it from me. I lay it down of my own accord" (John 10:18). While Jesus predicted that he would be "given over" into the "hands" of sinful men (Luke 9:44), at the last moment of his life, he reveals that there is another plan at work. Jesus himself—not the chief priests or Roman soldiers—is the one doing the final giving over of his life. "I commit my Spirit," he says. And he is not giving his life to his enemy's hand, but to the hand of his Father—a hand which the New Testament reveals is totally trustworthy and expresses God's providential care for his people (see John 10:29; Acts 4:28, 30). "Father, into your hands I commit my spirit" (Luke 23:46).

Finally, it is interesting that the psalm Jesus quotes—Psalm 31—was, according to later rabbinic tradition, used as an evening prayer asking God to protect his people when they slept. If the psalm was used in this way in Jesus' own time, then his prayer takes on even greater meaning. It is as if Jesus is about to enter the sleep of death and he is entrusting himself to the Father, who he believes will protect him during his "sleep" and vindicate him when he "awakens" in the Resurrection on the third day.

It's fitting, therefore, that Catholics around the world continue to use Psalm 31 as part of a beautiful liturgical devotion known as Night Prayer. Before going to sleep each night, clergy and religious around the world and many lay people as well pray Night Prayer and entrust themselves to the Father like Jesus did before he entered the sleep of death, saying, "Into your hands, Lord, I commit my spirit."

———————— **REFLECTION QUESTIONS** ————————

- *Before he dies, Jesus cries out, "Father, into your hands I commit my spirit" (Luke 23:46). How do these last words reveal Jesus is not a passive victim breathing his last breath, but the one in control of all the events on Good Friday? How might Jesus' example inspire us when we face challenges, setbacks, and sufferings in life?*

- *In what ways are you hesitant to entrust your life to the Father's hands? Are there certain areas of your life you want to keep in your own hands and not entrust to him? The Bible describes the "hands" of God the Father as totally trustworthy and caring for all our needs (see John 10:29; Acts 4:28). How might that help you?*

- *This book is called,* No Greater Love: A Biblical Walk Through Christ's Passion. *For as St. John Paul II once said, the passion of Christ is "the culmination of the revelation of God's love." What moment or theme in the Passion narratives struck you the most as revealing God's love?*

ABOUT THE AUTHOR

Dr. Edward Sri is a theologian, author, and well-known Catholic speaker who appears regularly on EWTN. Each year he speaks to clergy, parish leaders, catechists, and laity from around the world.

He has written several Catholic best-selling books, including *Men, Women and the Mystery of Love* (Servant); *A Biblical Walk Through the Mass* (Ascension); *Walking with Mary* (Image); and *Who Am I to Judge?: Responding to Relativism with Logic and Love* (Ignatius Press).

Edward Sri is the presenter of several popular faith formation programs, including *A Biblical Walk Through the Mass* (Ascension) *Mary: A Biblical Walk with the Blessed Mother* (Ascension); and *Follow Me: Meeting Jesus in the Gospel of John* (Ascension). He is also the host of the film series *Symbolon: The Catholic Faith Explained* (Augustine Institute).

He is a founding leader with Curtis Martin of FOCUS (Fellowship of Catholic University Students) and currently serves as FOCUS vice president of formation.

Dr. Sri is also the host of the weekly podcast *All Things Catholic* and leads pilgrimages to Rome and the Holy Land each year. He holds a doctorate from the Pontifical University of St. Thomas Aquinas in Rome and is an adjunct professor at the Augustine Institute. He resides with his wife Elizabeth and their eight children in Littleton, Colorado.

You can connect with Edward Sri through his website edwardsri.com or follow him on Facebook, Twitter, and Instagram.

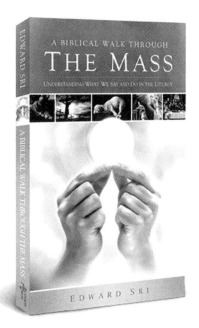